One
Good Year

· · · · · · · · · · · · · · · · · · · ·

of Marriage

LIFEMATES
SERIES

One Good Year

of Marriage

DR. DAVID & JANET CONGO

LIFE JOURNEY®

Bringing Home the Message for Life

An Imprint of Cook Communications Ministries • Colorado Springs, CO

Life Journey® is an imprint of
Cook Communications Ministries, Colorado Springs, CO 80918
Cook Communications, Paris, Ontario
Kingsway Communications, Eastbourne, England

ONE GOOD YEAR
© 2004 by Dr. David and Janet Congo

First Printing, 2004
Printed in United States of America
1 2 3 4 5 6 7 8 9 10 Printing/Year 08 07 06 05 04

Library of Congress Cataloging-in-Publication Data

Congo, David, 1946-
  One good year / by David and Janet Congo.
      p. cm.
Includes bibliographical references and index.
  ISBN 0-7814-3819-5
  1. Spouses--Religious life. 2. Middle aged persons--Religious life.
3. Marriage--Religious aspects--Christianity. I. Congo, Janet, 1949-
II. Title.
BV4596.M3C665 2004
248.8'44--dc22
                              2003024599

CONTENTS

Foreword 9

Introduction 11

MONTH #1 — ENCOURAGEMENT: Leaving Behind Destructive Criticism 19

MONTH #2 — INTENTIONAL CHOICE: Leaving Behind Complacency 31

MONTH #3 — FORGIVENESS: Leaving Behind Toxic Hurts .45

MONTH #4 — AWARENESS: Leaving Behind Apathy 61

MONTH #5 — BOUNDARIES: Leaving Behind Indifference .73

MONTH #6 — CONNECTION: Leaving Behind Distance 89

MONTH #7 — LAUGHTER: Leaving Behind Intensity 105

MONTH #8 — TEAMWORK: Leaving Behind the Power Struggle 117

MONTH #9 — FAITH: Leaving Behind Religion 133

MONTH #10 — SEXUALITY: Leaving Behind Monotony 151

MONTH #11 — BALANCE: Leaving Behind Instability 171

MONTH #12 — LEGACY: Leaving Behind Passivity 193

Notes 213

Mike and Lisa Keyes
Our friends for life,
Our partners in ministry.
Your faith, your creativity,
and your vision
challenge us.
Your relationships
inspire us!

FOREWORD

I'VE KNOWN JAN AND DAVE FOR OVER twenty years. From the outset I knew this was a couple to watch—they had something to offer—and they do. As founders of the highly creative LifeMates ministry they are impacting thousands of couples with their program and books.

I read the first chapter of their new book, *One Good Year*, and thought, "How practical! If the other chapters are like this one we have a winner." And they are!

This resource comes with handles, what you can do to change patterns that have crept in over the years and are starting to erode the relationship. You won't just read information, but you'll be interacting and thinking.

This book anticipates your questions and gives real solutions. In a time when there is an overabundance of books on marriage, *One Good Year* is a breath of fresh air. Read, learn, enjoy, and grow.

H. Norman Wright
Marriage, Family and Child Counselor and Author

INTRODUCTION

IF YOU HAVE PICKED UP THIS BOOK, most likely you have been married for several years.

Congratulations! That means you have survived "marriage" as you know it!

Moments of agony	Moments of ecstasy
Embarrassing moments	Unrealistic expectations
Treasured friendships	Monotonous moments
Multiple misunderstandings	Astounding surprises
Cold, stormy silences	Hot, fiery exchanges
Slightly veiled threats	Impatient sarcasm
Tearful tragedies	Accepted apologies
Extended family challenges	Tender touches
Unfortunate timing	Anxious times
Communication gridlock	Lonely times
Moments of deep connection	Moments of renewal
Shared insecurities	Mundane choices
Disappointing differences	Expressed gratitude
Exhilarating differences	Moments of connection
Moments of disconnection	Childish temper tantrums
Sizzling sexuality	Moments of grace
Eyeball-to-eyeball exchanges	Moments of hilarity

Where do you find your marriage after the multiple moments both of you have experienced together? Are you happily connected or hopelessly disconnected? If you have children, have they brought you closer to each other, or has child rearing left you distant from each other? Has your marriage turned into a business partnership dedicated to raising great kids, or have you maintained a thriving "us" over the years?

Starting Over

What do you think of when you hear the term, "starting over"? Does it leave you with a feeling of pessimism? Do you tell yourself, "Why bother, what's the use, we've tried so many times before"?

Often "starting over" means we whitewash our problems, close our eyes, avoid, ignore, and deny any difficulties. We say things like, "Problems? Who, us? We have a wonderful relationship." Frankly, that philosophy is akin to rearranging the deck chairs on the Titanic.

The truth is that we can change our unproductive patterns of interacting and repeating the same mistakes. We can reverse patterns leading to disillusionment.

Just like a lobster that regularly sheds its shell when it starts to feel cramped, periodically we need to admit that the way we are doing marriage isn't working anymore. Every couple could use one good year of marriage where they leave behind past failures, disappointments, and ineffective patterns. They can make new memories and establish new effective patterns. If you commit to work through the chapters of *One Good Year*, one month at a time, you will have experienced a great year of marriage!

In Need of a New Beginning

A warring couple sat with us in the counseling center. As they shared the pain of the last twenty years, it became obvious that they had established a pattern in their first year of marriage. In their attempt to solve the issue of in-law interference, they had gotten locked into a way of doing conflict. She pushed. He caved in and then resented her. He began to distance and detach. No matter what she tried, he was unreachable. Even though they had been married twenty years, basically they had only one year's experience of conflict resolution, which they then had repeated each year for twenty years.

Regardless of the years you have under your belt, regardless of the mistakes you have made and the pain you have inflicted, do you dare to shed that hard shell and risk vulnerability and the waves of change so that together you can have one really good year? Together you can grow into a new level of relationship that fits both of you better than anything you have encountered up to this time! If you are willing to take the risk and work at creating one good year of marriage, you can create a positive pattern and then repeat it each successive year. What a difference that could make in your marriage as you approach the next season of married life.

Rather than divorcing each other, we need to divorce the way we do marriage!

Relationship problems aren't solved by ending relationships. Those of us who have been married seven, fifteen, twenty-five, and forty years have faced our natural inclination to carry on the old patterns. After all, they are familiar. On one hand they're unfulfilling, but on the other hand they're comfortable. What if we started over? What dialogues would we need to have? What decisions might we need to make? What strengths would we have to own? What habits would we need to change?

One Good Year challenges a couple to walk into a whole new way of doing marriage. The goal is to remain committed to the marriage, to keep valuing each other, and to express love and respect while changing habits that don't help us achieve our goals. What your marriage was, it was. Now it's time to create what it can be! What would you like your marriage to look like one year from today?

Start Over: Release Unrealistic Expectations!

Even after being married a number of years, it's all too easy to idealize and romanticize love and marriage. Marriage is presented by some in the media as the primary vehicle for personal happiness, emotional satisfaction, and spiritual transformation. Our mates are somehow supposed to be capable, if they were only doing it "right," of making our world ideal.

Even though after seven or so years of marriage we have run into the solid wall of reality one too many times, it's still easy to harbor unrealistic expectations. So, when we run into a bump in the marital road, we fantasize that marriage should provide an ideal level of happiness and connectedness. We compare our harsh reality with that ideal fantasy. The fantasy wins 100 percent of the time.

Couples with satisfying long-term relationships will tell you that every marriage is composed of multiple moments—some of which are difficult, discouraging, and at times terribly disappointing. In fact, research (Institute for American Values study led by University of Chicago sociologist Linda Waite) has verified that almost 80 percent of couples who were "very unhappy" in their marriages and yet agreed not to divorce described themselves as "happy" five years later (*Wall Street Journal*, January 11, 2003). We can have marvelous moments of intimacy and connection and in the same relationship multiple moments of disconnection and distance.

People who refuse to release their expectation of the romantic ideal become critical, judgmental, accusing, and demanding. Yet when we are in touch with reality, we know that we are all unfinished, immature, and imperfect human beings. Couples who don't battle their unrealistic expectations end up battling each other.

Realize the Importance of Communication

The goal is not to imitate anyone else's marriage relationship; instead, discover together what works best for both of you and your relationship. Marriages and people need attention to thrive. After we've been married over seven years, it's easy to assume that there is nothing left to learn about our LifeMate. How wrong we are! Talking and listening for the purpose of learning are crucial choices for those choosing to start over.

Perhaps in the past when you sat down together as a couple to talk about the state of affairs in your marriage, you found yourself paralyzed. You weren't certain where to start. You didn't want to offend. The silence screamed at you. The anxiety was tangible. The children provided welcome interruptions. It felt so awkward that you decided it was easier not to ever try. So you gave up before you started.

One Good Year is designed to be an interactive guide to lead you in discussions with each other and in discovery of each other. We have chosen twelve issues around which couples frequently get stuck. Each chapter provides a guide for couple interaction around one of these issues. Read the chapters together; complete the personal inventories; pause in your reading for "heart-to-heart" talks. Explore four "Pillow Talks" or "Date Nights" at the end of each chapter, one for each week of the month. "Pillow Talks" give thoughtful conversation starters for genuine relationship building. "Date Nights" make sure you don't run out of ways to spend time with each other. By the time you have finished this book you will have left behind toxic patterns and adopted new effective patterns. If you will make the following twelve commitments your marriage will be transformed. The following twelve commitments will developed in the chapters of this book.

The Twelve Commitments of One Good Year

In my desire to live *One Good Year* of marriage with my LifeMate,

I commit on a daily basis to be an encouraging partner.
I commit to make intentional choices that enrich our marriage!
I commit to forgive and to be aware of my need for forgiveness.
I commit to practice awareness of my LifeMate on an ongoing basis.
I commit to protect the boundaries of our marriage.
I commit to connect in healthy ways on a daily basis.

I commit to making joy and laughter part of our relationship.

I commit on a daily basis to be a team player in our relationship.

I commit to making our spiritual relationship my highest priority.

I commit to making our sexual relationship satisfying, sensual, and
spiritual.

I commit to establishing balance in my marriage.

I commit to leaving a significant and eternal legacy!

Take a month to practice new habits and to implement new choices if need be. Don't race through the book. New choices only become habits after they have been successfully repeated one day at a time and one choice at a time. It's been said that it takes twenty-one days to start a new habit. We've designed this book so you have thirty days to implement change in one area of your marriage.

Recruit Support

If you are committing to embark on this adventure consider asking someone of the same sex to be your prayer and accountability partner. This is crucial. Choose a person who trusts God, who believes in marriage, and whom you respect. It is helpful if your partner is married or widowed. If possible, your support partner should be older than you. Consider these characteristics:

- someone who treats you as an adult capable of making your own decisions
- someone who doesn't shock easily, who doesn't judge or give you unasked for advice
- someone who is not embarrassed by your tears, who does not attack your character, and who does not spiritualize everything
- someone warm, affectionate, and approachable; vulnerable and free to share his or her times of difficulty with you; wise to discern the issues and help you recall your strengths when you have forgotten

them; trustworthy to keep commitments, promises and your confidences

- someone who will pray for you, with you, and for your marriage
- someone who is a source of encouragement, perspective, accountability, and wisdom
- someone who can provide a safe place to unload your feelings and to confess
- someone who will consistently support your commitment to your marriage and never slam your mate

Grace is hard to grasp. As Christians we may live in the land of no condemnation (Romans 8:1), but not until our weakness is known and loved by grace (unmerited favor) does it lose its power over us. How does this happen? James tells us, "Therefore confess your sins to each other and pray for each other so that you may be healed" (James 5:16).

STOP! We suggest that you don't go any further in this book until you have found your support person. Bottom line: Find a friend!

The Excitement of Starting Over

Few things bring more anticipation, joy, and excitement than choosing to make a new start. Whether it is starting out on a trip, embracing a new challenge at work, or letting go of some bad habits in marriage, we begin an adventure with no idea of the outcome. We feel hopeful, excited, and brave. We are changed by just the energy of the attempt.

When we change who we are, we change everything around us. Who knows—in one year, we may be able to create a whole new way of "doing marriage." Join your LifeMate and embark on the adventure of a lifetime. Together, why don't you both start over with that special person in your life?

M O N T H

ONE

"Encouragement: Leaving Behind Destructive Criticism"

> *"All those who have good ... wives (and) husbands ...*
> *may be sure that at some times ... they are loved*
> *not because they are loveable, but because Love*
> *Himself is in those who love them."*
>
> **C.S. Lewis**[1]

WE FEEL ENERGIZED BY ENCOURAGERS. They are mentors to us in many ways. They think the best of us, attribute the best intentions to our words and actions, and challenge us to be all that we can be. They respect us. They are positive, empowering, and transforming persons in our life journey. They help us to see the good in ourselves. It's as if they see a seed of potential in us and water it with acts of kindness and regular affirmations. We love to be in their presence.

When we are around an encourager, our step is a little lighter, we walk a little taller, and we even enjoy our own quirkiness a little more. An encourager comes alongside us and helps us dig through the dirt of failures and mistakes so that we learn from that experience. An encourager lifts us up when we fall down. When we are discouraged, the encourager challenges us to take one more step. An encourager is a true friend. An encourager is one of God's greatest blessings in our life. A LifeMate who makes it a personal goal to be the voice of encouragement becomes invaluable.

A critical spirit, on the other hand, makes a marriage brittle. We are left cut at the core, and love, rather than being strong and robust, becomes increasingly fragile and weak. An encouraging spirit, by contrast, provides a welcome retreat for any of us with battle scars from dealing with the world at large. A husband or wife can provide something for a LifeMate that is rarely found anywhere else—encouragement. If going home means that we will be encouraged and appreciated, which one of us wouldn't want to go home?

When we choose to be an encourager in our LifeMate's life, we give a priceless gift. It's much easier to encourage someone who sees the world as we see it; it's more challenging when it seems like we're coming from opposite ends of the spectrum in every encounter we have. How can we encourage someone who is so different from us?

Discourager: Doing What Comes Naturally

There wasn't just one bad apple in this marriage. Both Otis and Mary killed love by the way they talked to each other. They had failed to learn that a loving relationship is not built with a hammer.

While Mary was enjoying an early morning aerobics class at the gym one Saturday, Otis was on breakfast duty. He and his two teenage boys went all out as they made breakfast together. They prepared waffles with strawberries, whipped cream, sausage, and eggs. Immediately following breakfast, the three of them went outside to shoot a few baskets—leaving total chaos in the kitchen.

Mary drove in the driveway to be greeted by three sweaty, happy, laughing guys. However, when she walked into the kitchen she almost had a heart attack. She yelled at Otis, "What do you take me for anyway, your slave? I suppose you think I have nothing better to do today but pick up after you slobs. Get in here immediately!"

Otis slammed the ball onto the driveway. He looked at his sons and said, "Your mom is wigging out again." With a roll of his eyes he headed into the kitchen. He slammed the door, glared at Mary with disgust and yelled back, "What is wrong with you? You jump to conclusions. I never said I wouldn't clean this up. You always overreact."

Mary fired back, "If I didn't get upset this kitchen would never get cleaned up. You're just an overgrown jock. You're a lousy example to our sons. You don't take any responsibility. You're just like your dad. All he did on Saturdays was sports. It's hopeless to be on our sons' backs to clean up after themselves when you don't clean up after yourself."

> "Lord, give me the heart to see my LifeMate through your eyes."

That was more than Otis wanted to hear, "Well, if it isn't little Miss Perfect yelling. Bet you don't talk to that trainer at the gym or your church friends like that. Wish I had a videotape. You're such a hypocrite. What a witch!"

With those arrows flying, Otis picked up some plates and plunked them down on the counter. Mary glared at him and stomped out.

Otis mumbled something and yelled at his sons to come in and put their dishes in the dishwasher. The three of them practically threw the dirty dishes into the appliance. Otis cleaned up the counters and then went outside to shoot some more hoops.

Mary returned to the kitchen. She was still on a roll. She picked up the dishcloth, let out a loud sigh and yelled once more at Otis, "You call this a clean counter? Are you blind? There are crumbs all over the counter and on the floor. What's wrong with you? I have to do all the work around here myself …"

Otis shook his head, ground his teeth, and missed the basket! A Saturday morning is ruined. A couple is stuck.

From Jan's Journal

I came into our marriage with a need to be right and with a competitive streak that demonstrated itself verbally. I'm not proud of either of these traits. David, on the other hand, valued our relationship more than he valued "rightness."

I learned fairly early in our marriage that because I was quicker in my verbal skills, I could verbally assassinate Dave and leave him lying in a pool of blood. He'd withdraw to nurse his wounds. I'd feel "right" and as if I'd "won" this one. I'd even feel self-righteous about my anger. Over the years, I've learned that there is little in life that is more destructive than anger voiced with a lack of self-discipline and given with a self-righteous attitude.

One day we'd had one of these all-too-familiar altercations. They made me feel temporarily powerful, I'm ashamed to say. This day instead of patting myself on the back, I looked into David's eyes. At that moment I saw what I was doing to our love. At the same time I became acutely aware that when I had intimidated this guy I said I loved, I had been dishonest. I hadn't let Dave see my heart. I hadn't spoken my truth. The truth was I was afraid. I was hurt, and I was terrified of being controlled. My attempts to keep from being controlled turned me into a reactive controller.

My reactivity and my sharp tongue had in no way helped me to know my husband nor to disclose who I was. That day I became aware that my uncensored expressions of thoughts and feelings were not honest. They were reactive, familiar, and immature. It was the opposite of my value system. I came to see that timing, tact, and kindness are not dishonest. They make honesty possible.

For the first time in our marriage I went to my husband with a truly repentant attitude and asked for his forgiveness. He gave it. He was more interested in the relationship than in being "right."

Heart2Heart

1. **What are the choices both Otis and Mary made that kept their negative cycle going?**

2. **What could Mary have done differently so that Saturday morning wasn't ruined?**

3. **Even if Mary blew it, how could Otis have responded differently?**

Have you ever had a moment of self-revelation like this—a time when you realized you were worried about the speck in your LifeMate's eye while you had a log in your own? Try this "logectomy." Each of you can take this personal inventory separately. Put a check mark by any of the following statements that are true of you.

Him Her

_____ _____ I find it hard to accept my LifeMate's differences.

_____ _____ I find it hard to forgive my LifeMate for not living up to my expectations.

_____ _____ I feel critical of my LifeMate at least three times a week.

_____ _____ When I am upset I use my mouth as a weapon to make my LifeMate feel small.

_____ _____ When I am upset I tell my LifeMate what he or she is thinking.

_____ _____ When I am upset I often act as an amateur therapist pointing out my LifeMate's current dysfunction.

_____ _____ When I am upset I tune out my LifeMate and disengage from the conversation.

_____ _____ When I am upset, I threaten to leave.

_____ _____ When I am upset I use the words "always" and "never" frequently.

_____ _____ When I am upset I bring up my LifeMate's failures.

_____ _____ When I am upset I immediately become mean-spirited. I use name calling, sneering, hostile humor, and sarcasm to demean my LifeMate.

_____ _____ When I am upset I consistently use the word "You" followed by a critical, attacking put-down.

_____ _____ When I am upset I wait for my LifeMate to come forward with an apology. I rarely if ever make any attempt at repairing the relationship.

What did you learn about yourself by completing the questionnaire? If you checked the majority of these statements, you are a tremendously unsafe person for your LifeMate to deal with. In fact, you have become an intimate terrorist in your home. Each of us must be more deeply concerned about our own attitudes than our LifeMate's issues. If you dare, have your LifeMate take the above questionnaire on you! Franklin D. Roosevelt said, "It is better to swallow words than to have to eat them later."[2]

> It is better to swallow words than to have to eat them later!
>
> Franklin D. Roosevelt
>
> (Sam Horn, Tongue Fu. St Martin's Press, New York, 1996, p.48)

New Choices

All married people get angry and frustrated with their LifeMate. Most of the frustrations and irritations of learning to live with an ever-changing human being don't kill love. However, the consistent habit of making your LifeMate feel small, minimized, and demeaned does. Each of us should come with a warning label. If we aren't intentional in this area, in a fit of passionate anger we will do what comes naturally. Our habitually patterned behavior will destroy love.

If these have been your choices in the past, you are suffering from the misconception that marriage is a reform school. It is not! The only person you can change is yourself, and that is difficult enough. Ask the apostle Paul (Romans 7:15–16, 24–25).

Transition to Becoming an Encourager!

Interactions in relationships are circular. You do or say something. … Your LifeMate responds or reacts. … You respond or counter (ups the ante). … Your LifeMate responds or counters (ups the ante) … .

We can interrupt the cycle by responding rather than reacting! A critical spirit will not get me what I want! Perfection is not the goal. If all I can imagine is a perfectly loving, respectful, romantic, and soulful adventure when I say the word "marriage," I have just set myself up for despair.

Everything will not come up rosy all the time. All marriages have ups and downs. Occasionally there are bumps in the road. Most couples who make it their goal to stop making their LifeMate feel small say that their rough moments become shorter in duration, less intense, and less frequent. Rough moments are to be expected. They provide an opportunity for growth. Even in the best marriages, people have bad breath, they get short with one another, they pout, they resent doing chores, and they have bad hair days.

Choose Your Direction

Consider how you respond to criticism:

- **Turn Inward:** I feel defensive, deflated, and demoralized. If past mistakes have been brought up I am left focused on what I did wrong, which increases the chances that I will repeat the same mistakes.
- **Turn Against:** I fire back a criticism or threaten to leave, while fantasizing about being married to someone who appreciates me.
- **Turn Away:** I withdraw and nurse my wounds, afraid of another conflict, and feel victimized by my LifeMate's words.

There is another option even if your LifeMate blows it! You can choose to **Turn Toward** your LifeMate! Here are a few ways to do that.

- **Say "OUCH!"** If your LifeMate has zapped you with critical words, say something like this: "OUCH! When you call me _____, I feel unloved and devalued. Is that what you intended?"

Heart2Heart

1. Complete this statement using the information from the previous "logectomy" questionnaire and from your LifeMate's input.

   In the past when we have had an argument, I believe I have been unsafe to you in these specific ways. … Would you agree?

2. Where did you first develop your destructive habits? Is this the way your parents treated each other or you? Did you develop these in a particularly hurtful relationship?

3. As you look over the questionnaire, what are one or two choices you want to change so that you can be more of an encourager?

- **Ask for a Do-Over!** "We agreed that calling each other names kills our love, so I'd like to ask you to do-over what you just said."

- **Take a Time-Out!** If your LifeMate doesn't stop the critical words and you begin to feel uncomfortable with where the interaction is going, you can say, "This conversation doesn't feel good to me. I need to take a time-out." In that case it is important that both of you stop the conversation immediately. Each of you has an hour to cool off prior to attempting the discussion again. After the hour, if you need a longer period to cool down, ask for it. Notice that you are admitting your own personal need for a time-out; you are in no way attempting to control your LifeMate.

- **Admit Your Part.** If you slip back into a critical spirit, catch yourself immediately. You might say something like this, "I am sorry for reacting. I want to speak to you with respect. I need to redo that."

Commit to STOP using destructive criticism as a tool for promoting change. It never works. Your LifeMate may do what you want temporarily, but he or she will resent you for it. Instead you might say, "When I have been upset, I have made choices that made you feel disrespected. I have_____. This is a destructive pattern that hurts you, me, and our love. If something you do upsets me, I will ask for what I need by using positive, specific, action requests. If you are unable to give me what I need, I will ask you why. If I slip back into old habits, point them out to me, and I will rephrase my request."

A Scriptural Challenge!

"Finally, all of you, live in harmony with one another; be sympathetic, love as brothers, be compassionate and humble. Do not repay evil with evil or insult with insult, but with blessing, because to this you were called so that you may inherit a blessing. For,

'Whoever would love life
 and see good days
must keep his tongue from evil

and his lips from deceitful speech.

He must turn from evil and do good;

he must seek peace and pursue it.

For the eyes of the Lord are on the

righteous

And his ears are attentive to their

prayer,

But the face of the Lord is against

those who do evil.'"

1 Peter 3:8–12

Four tremendous benefits come from choosing to encourage, or to bless. These are laid out in the verses above.

1. When we give, we get (verse 9).

In what ways might you be encouraged personally if you became intentional about speaking words of encouragement to your LifeMate? Has this ever happened to you?

2. Our days are free of the tension and stress that bitterness and resentment cause (verse 10).

Give details about a time in your life when you increased your stress as a result of having a critical spirit. Did you learn anything from that experience?

3. Our prayers will be answered (verse 12).

Has there been a time in your marriage or in your life when you have dealt with someone else's critical comment in a way that didn't result in you imitating them? What happened?

4. God will deal with the person who is insulting us (verse 12).

The principle of rendering a blessing for an insult is common thread throughout the New Testament. Take the time to look up these New

Heart2Heart

1. How could we adapt these four suggestions to our marriage so they move us both in the direction of being encouragers?

2. What are five toxic words or phrases that we would like to drop from our marriage repertoire? Write them down.

3. What do you find most challenging to encourage about your LifeMate?

Testament verses in the next month:

Matthew 5: 43–47	1 Corinthians 4:12
Luke 6:28	1 Thessalonians 5:15
Romans 12:17–21	

Start Over as an Encourager!

Love always needs an opportunity for a new start! In a long-term marriage it is far too easy to overvalue what someone is not and to undervalue who he or she is. What's the secret of giving positive feedback year after year after year? Adjust your attitude from focusing on what is wrong to focusing on what is right! Practice noticing behaviors and interactions that you like and admire. Use these observations to give credibility and power to your statements of encouragement. Saying, "I love you!" gets you a grade of "B+." Saying, "I love this specific thing about you" gets you an "A+"!

Rate yourself on the following scale in reference to your level of connection. Where do you see yourself on this continuum? Share with your LifeMate.

Red Zone	Yellow Zone	Green Zone
I consistently make my mate feel small.	When I'm upset, I use my tongue to hurt. When I'm not, I use my tongue to encourage.	I am an encourager. I am careful about my words.

Four men responded to the statement "The best thing about being married is …" with these words:

"I actually love cooking for my wife. It is nice to have an appreciative guinea pig who is willing to suffer as I try to remember what the heck the Naked Chef put in that sauce last night."

"There is nothing better than waking up next to my wife. We always squeeze in some extra snuggles before we have to drag ourselves out of bed, and somehow that cozy start makes facing the rest of the day just a little bit easier."

"What I love most about being married is that I have someone to share the big decisions with: I always turn to my wife for her opinion and support. I recently quit my job and started my own business, and having someone to listen and act as a sounding board made it easier to take such a scary risk. It's still nerve-racking, but I feel better knowing that my wife will be there for me no matter what happens."

"My wife has smelled my morning breath, watched me go bald, and heard all my boring stories—and she still thinks I'm the hottest guy in the world. You can't beat that!"

How would you complete the following sentence?

The best thing about marriage is_____.

Week 1: Pillow Talk

1. What is the most meaningful affirmation that your LifeMate could make about you in front of other people (your children included)?
2. When do you feel most supported by your LifeMate? When do you feel most respected?
3. Write down five qualities of your LifeMate that you have come to value over the years. If you can come up with more than five, great!

Week 2: Pillow Talk

1. Pretend that you are describing your LifeMate to someone who has never met him or her. Which physical features do you mention? Which character qualities do you highlight?
2. What do you see as your LifeMate's greatest talents and strengths?
3. What are some positive things other people have said about your LifeMate?

Week 3: Pillow Talk

1. What would you view as a physical expression of encouragement? (Some couples view holding hands or a pat on the rear as a gesture of encouragement. What about you?)

2. In what ways would you like to be encouraged by your LifeMate? What would you like him or her to notice? What are you proud of?

3. How would you complete this statement: "The thing I enjoy most about my LifeMate is…."?

   HINT: Exchange pictures of each other as children. Use these photos to remind yourselves that we each have a fragile, vulnerable self in need of honest encouragement.

Week 4: Pillow Talk

1. What are the things that work in your marriage? What do you value about your relationship? Write these down.

2. What is the most encouraging thing your LifeMate could say or do this next week? Have you in any way been surprised by your LifeMate's response to your encouragement?

3. What specific areas of your LifeMate's life could you pray that the Lord will bless?

IN MY DESIRE TO LIVE ONE GOOD YEAR OF MARRIAGE WITH MY LIFEMATE

I COMMIT ON A DAILY BASIS
TO BE AN ENCOURAGING PARTNER.

M O N T H

TWO

"Intentional Choice:
Leaving Behind Complacency"

> *"What you do speaks so loudly*
> *that I cannot hear what you say!"*
>
> **Ralph Waldo Emerson**[1]

WHY SHOULD WE CHOOSE WHAT IS BEST for our
LifeMate even when he or she doesn't deserve it? Because this is the
kind of person we want to be. Values motivate us to give more of ourselves than seems "fair." When we make intentional choices we choose
to live out of our value system. We cannot be true to ourselves without
being true to our values. Intentionality in attitude and action trans-
forms a relationship.

Dependency gets in the way of love. A dependent person relies heav-
ily on a LifeMate, relying on the spouse to do what the dependent spouse

is unable or unwilling to do. By contrast, an intentional LifeMate is aware of how important personal choices are to the domestic, romantic, financial, spiritual, social, and intimate aspects of marriage. An intentional LifeMate initiates loving actions even when the feelings of love are temporarily blocked.

When both LifeMates intentionally use their freedom to give to, to serve, and to love the other, their relationship is rejuvenated. In 1 Corinthians 13:5 Paul writes that love "is not self-seeking." An intentional marriage is a 100/100 proposition. Acts of service know no gender lines.

Intentional LifeMates are aware that the most important work of marriage is to help each other become all that they can possibly be. You care that your LifeMate lives out his or her value system and achieves personal goals. An intentional marriage supports the process of each other's growth.

Feelings of love flow from consistent acts of love.

The All-Too-Average Couple!

It's all too easy to get complacent; Dawn and Tyler could attest to that. It seemed as if all their efforts were directed toward their adolescent kids or friends who needed help. When they weren't at work, their together time consisted mostly of daily grind activities. They paid bills, arranged schedules, and did chores. It just seemed impossible to carve out couple time.

Once in a while, they went out together, but most of those times were shared with friends. When they did date each other, they rarely planned ahead of time what they would do. They usually wore grubbies. They might spend twenty minutes deciding what movie to see, but they'd often throw in the towel when they couldn't agree. Usually that scenario ended with the two of them watching different television programs in different rooms and sleeping in separate beds.

It seemed to both Dawn and Tyler over the years that it was easier to be nice to others than it was to be kind to each other. Dawn felt like she was expected to pay because Tyler worked and she was a full-time mom. Tyler seemed to give her a failing grade for every aspect of her life, from how she spent her time, to her grocery shopping style, to the meals she created for the family, to the way she spent money. Since Tyler worked out of the home he felt he shouldn't have to help around the house. Rarely if ever did he express gratitude for what Dawn did for him. His attitude was, "It's about time you do something around here."

Dawn's reaction was to resent Tyler. She told her friends what a jerk he was. They sympathized with her: "It must be difficult to be married to him." She made sarcastic comments to their adult children about their dad. She fluctuated between depression and anger. She did less and less around the house. She spent more and more time at the church and with friends and fantasized about the empty nest stage when she'd go to school and get a career. She didn't want to ever be financially dependent on Tyler again. Dawn's schedule was full; her love tank was empty.

> ## Heart2Heart
>
> **What choices had Tyler and Dawn neglected that resulted in the pain they were both feeling right now?**
>
> **In what specific ways has the germ of complacency become a virus in your relationship?**
>
> **How would you like your relationship to be different? Be specific.**

From Jan's Journal:

About fifteen years ago I had the privilege of attending a seminar by Emilie Barnes. I came away from this enjoyable experience with a great idea. She suggested that every couple needs a "love basket."

A love basket is a basket that holds a tablecloth, candles, matches, napkins, silverware, and plates. It can be packed by either sex. It is never to be used with friends or with children. It is to be used to enjoy time with your LifeMate alone.

This was a great idea for me because I love to create experiences. I got busy and went shopping looking for the right items. Eventually I found them and the love basket was complete. Now the issue was when was I going to surprise David with it?

At that time, he was working forty hours a week in addition to carrying a full-time doctoral program. It had been quite a few weeks since we'd had some significant heart-to-heart time. I phoned the secretary at the office where he worked and asked her to book me into David's schedule as a new client. I even invented a new name. The secretary promised to keep my secret.

At the appointed time, I arrived at Dave's office, love basket and all. Dave was shocked to see me sitting in the waiting room, but he quickly recovered his composure. I confessed my covert plan and then we had a fabulous hour together in his office. He said it made his week.

That love basket has been to the beach, to libraries, to museums, to art galleries, on bike trips, hiking excursions, camping trips, and every so often just enjoyed in our bedroom.

"We make a living by what we get, but we make a life by what we give."

Winston Churchill

(Richardson, Cheryl, Life Makeovers, Broadway Books, New York, 2000, page 185.)

When we conduct a marriage retreat, we share the love basket idea. Periodically we hear reports of delightful times couples have shared over a love basket. A few years ago we got a report from a couple who had made their love basket an important part of their relationship. They had been going through a personally devastating time. One of them had been laid off from work, a parent had died, another parent was in the early stages of Alzheimer's, and they were questioning whether they would have to declare bankruptcy. College for their daughters was looming ahead. What were they to do?

Their adolescent daughters were fifteen and seventeen. One evening the girls greeted their parents as they came through the door. The girls told them that they would be at a friend's home for a sleepover. They said that there was a surprise for their parents in the living room. With that the girls left, overnight bags and all. The parents walked into the living room, and there in front of the roaring fireplace was a blanket with an overflowing love basket sitting on it. They had forgotten to take time alone together in the midst of life's curveballs, but their adolescent daughters had remembered.

From Dave's Journal:

When I was taking my doctorate I was working forty hours a week as well as taking a full load of graduate classes. Unfortunately, the reality was that I had little time for Jan and Christopher. Often there would be an exam on a Friday morning, and that had to have my undivided attention when I finally came home at night.

> Romance is the 'Show and Tell' of love!

Around Thursday evening Jan would get frustrated because all week I had been so unavailable to her and to our son. Instead of demonstrating a temporary moment of maturity, she'd be human and express her frustration to me with a question like, "Don't you even care about me and Christopher?"

Well, that would get my attention. I felt guilty. I would pull myself away from my books for a few moments, but I was still not totally there with her and Christopher. In the back of my mind I was pressured about the exam. Furthermore, it was less than satisfying for Jan, since she felt I was only there because she had made a scene, not because I really wanted to be with my family.

After this happened several times, we decided to adopt a habit that radically affected our relationship. On Sunday evening we sat down with an empty master calendar for the coming week. We discussed our priorities and put them on the calendar first. Couple time got top billing. If my reality involved one of those weeks with an exam on Friday I would put couple time after the exam on Friday evening. That way Jan knew time together was a priority of mine. It would still be a full week, but we both could anticipate time together on Friday evening.

Transition Toward Intentional Choice in My Value System

What are you like in public? What are you like at home? Could a stranger follow the two of you around for a week and know, without your telling him, by looking at your lifestyle, your choices, the expenditure of your time, money, and energy what your value system and your goals were? Is your marriage a living demonstration of the values you both hold?

- What qualities do you want to be known for at the end of your life? Every interaction between you and your LifeMate becomes an opportunity to live out of your value system.
- On a regular basis, we need to ask ourselves these questions. You might even decide that each of you should discuss them with your support person.
- In our last conflict did I live and respond according to who I want to be … a person grounded in my values? Explain.
- When I am stressed and overburdened, do I live out of my value system? Explain.
- When there is tension between us, do I live out of my value system? Explain.
- When I refuse to do something to lighten my LifeMate's load, am I living out of my values? Explain.
- What excuses do I give for failing to live out my value system? Be specific.
- Do I ever use my LifeMate's strengths to grow? How?
- Do I ever use his or her weaknesses to stay true to my values and to pursue personal growth? The "usual" way to handle your LifeMate's weaknesses is to ignore them or to humiliate your LifeMate because of them.
- What would I need to change about my own behavior in my marriage in order to be intentional about living out of my value system?

Even when everything around us is in change or crisis, we can cling to our value system. It never changes. In the following personal inventory, choose five values and ideals that you would want someone to use to describe you:

_____ Love

_____ Joy

_____ Peace

_____ Patience

_____ Goodness

_____ Self-control

_____ Availability

_____ Service

_____ Understanding

_____ Faith

_____ Wisdom

_____ Humor

_____ Charity

_____ Courage

_____ Tolerance

_____ Stability

_____ Flexibility

_____ Attentiveness

_____ Other _____

_____ Compassion

_____ Creativity

_____ Hospitality

_____ Gentleness

_____ Faithfulness

_____ Kindness

_____ Generosity

_____ Competence

_____ Moderation

_____ Hope

_____ Integrity

_____ Personal Strength

_____ Mercy

_____ Trust

_____ Empathy

_____ Optimism

_____ Equality

_____ Tact

Heart2Heart

Share your answers to the personal inventory with your LifeMate. Ask your LifeMate if there are specific ways that you can encourage him to live according to his top five values.

Combine your two lists of top five values. Is there any overlap? These are the mutually shared values that guide your life as a married couple. Ask your support people to pray that as you maintain an intentional awareness of these values you both hold, the Holy Spirit will grow you into that kind of person.

Did either of you learn something new about your LifeMate when you looked at each other's values?

A Scriptural Prayer of Thanksgiving

"I thank my God every time I remember you. … being confident of this, that he who began a good work in you will carry it on to completion until the day of Christ Jesus. … And this is my prayer: that your love may abound more and more in knowledge and depth of insight, so that you may be able to discern what is best and may be pure and blameless until the day of Christ, filled with the fruit of righteousness that comes through Jesus Christ—to the glory and praise of God" (Phil. 1:3, 6, 9–11).

Transition Toward Intentional Choice in My Actions

Periodically every marriage suffers from a case of the relationship "blahs." Nothing is terribly wrong, but nothing is particularly right either. You find yourselves simply too busy, too tired, or too stressed to relate effectively.

That's when we need to remind ourselves of some math facts. Five minutes devoted to romance equals one day of harmony. This is called the "5 to 1 principle."[2] Another math fact they didn't teach us in school is that 80 percent of the results in your relationship come from 20 percent of your effort.[3]

Check yourselves on the following statements. Let this serve as a reminder of these principles.

Daily Checklist

_____ I expressed my love to my LifeMate in words today.

_____ I checked in with my LifeMate one time during the day.

_____ I was affectionate with my LifeMate today (held hands, gave hugs, cuddled without pushing for anything else).

_____ I let my LifeMate know specific things I appreciated at least twice today.

_____ I spent at least fifteen minutes of uninterrupted time with my LifeMate sharing the positive things that happened in my day.

_____ I lightened my LifeMate's load today, in one specific way, without being asked.

_____ Today I kissed my LifeMate hello and good-bye.

Weekly Checklist

_____ I planned a date time with my LifeMate.

_____ I sat down with my LifeMate to discuss our marriage and family issues.

_____ I made love with my LifeMate.

_____ I left a card or a love note somewhere where my LifeMate would find it.

_____ I expressed my gratitude for my LifeMate to someone else—his or her family or to one of his or her friends.

_____ I prayed with my LifeMate about our marriage and family.

_____ I facilitated my LifeMate's need for at least two hours of personal time.

Monthly Checklist

_____ I planned one romantic surprise.

_____ I rented a movie we both would enjoy.

_____ I made plans for a weekend get-a-way sometime in the next three months.

_____ I took my LifeMate out to dinner at least once.

_____ I brought home one small unexpected gift.

_____ I reminisced with my LifeMate about something romantic from our past with each other.

_____ I gave my LifeMate at least one all-over body massage and then let him/her rest.

A Calendar Date: Living on Purpose

On Sunday evening we sit down with a master calendar of the week. The first items that go on our calendar are some scheduled couple times. Then, when we have scheduled these significant couple times, we schedule the other events and activities that fill the rest of the week. Listed below are the other activities that get top billing on our calendar. Don't assume that you need to mimic us. Create your own times of connection.

- A date time once a week. Alternate the planning.
- A time of daily connection. Set aside twenty minutes a day to share a cup of tea. Discuss the interesting things that happened in your

Heart2Heart

Write out a prayer thanking God for your LifeMate. Ask Jesus to grow your LifeMate into the person he or she wants to be (refer back to your LifeMate's personal inventory to make your prayer specific). Ask the Holy Spirit to help form those values in your LifeMate's life. Acknowledge that you are willing to encourage your LifeMate on his or her journey. Ask the Lord to help you to use every interaction the two of you have to grow you into the person he wants you to be.

Read the prayer you have written to your LifeMate. Exchange prayers. Put the prayer in a place where you can read it once a day all month long.

day. Put some beautiful music on. Relax. Turn off the TV. This is a time to "touch one another's heart" without necessarily "touching one another's parts."

- A time for sexual intimacy and pleasuring. If it happens more than once during the week, great! It's a super week.
- A weekly issue discussion time. Two thirty- to sixty-minute time slots to discuss tough issues. We each get one time slot a week if needed. That way our problems aren't discussed every day, all day, polluting an entire week. Obviously there are times of crisis that can't wait for these scheduled times. We try not to make everything a crisis.
- A daily prayer time together.

Heart**2**Heart

Rate yourself on the scale at right in reference to your level of connection. Where do you see yourself on this continuum? Share with your LifeMate.

Red Zone	Yellow Zone	Green Zone
I do not initiate anything to enrich our marriage.	I do some things but I want to do more.	I am intentional. I look for opportunities to enrich our relationship.

Random Ideas to Make Your Marriage Happy!

Do something out of the ordinary!

- Write a love letter or poem to your LifeMate. Take some time to put your feelings down on paper. When you have completed it, frame it or wrap it in a gift box.
- Create your own David Letterman list: The Top Ten Reasons Why I Love You Are … .
- Create a calendar for one month of the year, perhaps your LifeMate's birthday month. Once a week put a surprise on the calendar (I will make your favorite dessert for dinner. I want to take you to a movie of your choice. You're entitled to a sensuous body massage, etc.)

On the other days write down one characteristic that you admire, love, or respect about your LifeMate.

• Create a gratitude journal. Once a day for a year catch your LifeMate doing something that you value, admire, love, or respect. Write down in a journal how much that means to you. At the end of the year give it to your LifeMate as a gift.

• Give your LifeMate a gift of your time and energy. Offer them a day (gift certificate included) that you will work on a project that is important to them or free them up for a day so they can spend time with friends and so forth.

Feelings of love flow from consistent acts of love. It isn't the bad stuff, but rather the lack of good stuff that causes complacency. The million-dollar question in a marriage is, "How can we increase the number of positive moments that we share?" One day a ham radio operator overheard an older gentleman giving this advice to a younger man on the air.

"It's a shame you have to be away from home and your family so much," he said. "Let me tell you something that has helped me keep a good perspective on my own priorities. You see, one day I sat down and did a little arithmetic. The average person lives about 75 years. Now then, I multiplied 75 times 52 and came up with 3,900, which is the number of Saturdays that the average person has in his lifetime.

"It took me until I was 55 years old to think about all this in any detail," he continued, "and by that time I had lived through over 2,800 Saturdays. I got to thinking that if I lived to be 75, I only had about a thousand of them left to enjoy."

He went on to explain that he bought 1,000 marbles and put them in a clear plastic container in his favorite work area at home. "Every Saturday since then," he said, "I have taken one marble out and thrown it away. I found that by watching the marbles diminish, I focused more on the really important things in life. There's nothing like watching your time here on this earth run out to help get your priorities straight."

Then the older gentleman finished. "Now let me tell you one last thought before I sign off and take my lovely wife out to breakfast. This morning, I took the very last marble out of the container. I figure if I make it until next Saturday, then I have been given a little extra time."[4]

Week 1: Pillow Talk

1. Make a list of all the interests and activities that you and your LifeMate have enjoyed over the lifetime of your marriage. Include small doable acts that don't have a big price tag that will warm your LifeMate's heart.

2. How could you re-create some of these wonderful times? (Visit the place where you met. Watch family videos. Return to special vacation spots, etc.)

3. As you reminisce, are there old friends whom you haven't contacted for quite a while? Make plans to call them and have a conference call, or make plans to do something with them that you would both enjoy.

Week 2: Pillow Talk

1. What interests does your LifeMate enjoy that you don't find appealing? List these interests. Exchange lists. Choosing to do something that your LifeMate enjoys is a love gift. Your attitude is crucial! If you can't find anything else redeemable about the activity, at least enjoy watching your LifeMate's enjoyment.

2. Put two of these activities on your calendar so that they are scheduled to happen in the next few months. Each of you choose one activity.

3. How has your LifeMate broadened your horizons? How have his or her separate interests stretched you out of your comfort zone?

Week 3: Date Night

1. Pretend that you are on vacation in your own town or city. Visit spots that you have preciously ignored. Visit bookstores, art galleries, museums, restaurants, or other points of interest. Your curiosity is the limit.

Why don't you pack a picnic dinner in a love basket? Pretend you are from out of town and explore together.

Week 4: Date Night

1. What kinds of PDA (public displays of affection) are you each comfortable with? Talk to each other about your preferences. Where do you think these come from?

2. Bring along a calendar for a year. Once a month plan to celebrate a romantic day or evening. Once in a while it might even be a weekend. Create a list together of some of the activities you might enjoy doing. Schedule these on your calendar. Alternate the planning of these times.

FROM PREVIOUS MONTH:

I COMMIT ON A DAILY BASIS

TO BE AN ENCOURAGING PARTNER.

**IN MY DESIRE TO LIVE ONE GOOD YEAR
OF MARRIAGE WITH MY LIFEMATE,**

I COMMIT TO MAKE INTENTIONAL CHOICES
THAT ENRICH OUR MARRIAGE!

MONTH

THREE

"Forgiveness: Leaving Behind Toxic Hurts"

> *"Lord, while we are changing patterns in our marriage that haven't been mutually beneficial. ... Help us each day to renew our commitment to our marriage vows and each other. Help us to keep short accounts so that hurts don't define our relationship. Help us to express and demonstrate love, respect, grace, and truth to each other in tangible ways every day. Thank you, Lord!"*

NO MARRIAGE CAN EXIST LONG WITHOUT tension, conflict, hurt, pain and injury, misunderstanding, suffering, and alienation. This is reality. So forgiveness is a necessary ongoing part of a committed, long-term relationship. Forgiveness becomes necessary when we have been dealt a hand we didn't choose.

You have heard the phrase, "love means never having to say you are sorry." Not true! Instead, love means you need to say you are sorry on an ongoing basis. Knowingly or unknowingly, we do or say things that hurt each other. We need forgiveness to move ahead successfully.

In the book, *LifeMates: A Lover's Guide for a Lifetime Relationship* (Cook Communications, 2002) we compare a married couple to two porcupines living in Alaska. When winter comes and the snow begins to fall, the porcupines feel cold and begin to draw closer together to keep warm. The result, however, is that they poke each other with their quills. When they separate, they become cold again. The dilemma is they want to be close, but they end up regularly experiencing discomfort and getting poked when they get close.

> A good marriage is the union of two forgivers!
>
> Ruth Bell Graham
>
> (Ronald Shwartz, The 501 Best and Worst Things Ever Said About Marriage, Citadel Press, New York, 1995, p 49)

We can't be married without getting poked! Not one of us is perfect. The writer of Ecclesiastes was in touch with reality when he wrote these words in Ecclesiastes 7:20: "There is not a righteous man on earth who does what is right and never sins." We regularly let each other down. We fail each other. In our hurt, we distance or we attack.

Forgiveness is not a one-time occurrence in marriage. It is a gradual process of increasing compassion and reducing resentment as we continue to forgive. Forgiveness draws us toward each other again. The past stays in the past because we have come to terms with it. In the present, we are released from an array of negative emotions such as fear, anger, suspicion, loneliness, and alienation. Forgiveness frees us to face our tomorrows confident that we're not lugging past luggage into it.

Forgiveness halts the cycle of blame and pain, breaking the chain imprisoning us. Forgiveness gives our relationship new life. Because of it we can interact authentically. Forgiveness is a gift we give ourselves, our LifeMates, and our marriages.

A Toxic Heart

Lashelle and Ken had been married thirty-five years. They had raised an outstanding family of four. All of their children were married and involved in ministry of some kind. They loved the grandparent stage and embraced it with great gusto. From the outside, everything seemed wonderful, but both Lashelle and Ken knew there was a cancer in their relationship.

Over the years, Lashelle had rejected Ken's affectionate and sexual advances on an ever-increasing basis. Eight years ago they would make love once or twice a month, but gradually that pattern changed. It had been five years since they had shared sexual intimacy at all.

Ken was upset about this reality. Sometimes he'd make snide, sarcastic comments to Lashelle about her weight. He'd be short and impatient with her. She'd react to his barbs by withdrawing into her happy world of children and grandchildren. She quietly resented Ken and wondered what it would be like to live alone. She'd greet Ken with a scowl when he returned home from work, criticize him for watching sports on television, and attack him for leaving his shoes around the house. She also complained that he was not the leader she wanted him to be. He'd react and stomp out of the house.

They were considering separation when Lashelle literally woke up in the middle of the night. She'd been dreaming about their courtship, something she hadn't thought about for a long time. They'd been so in love, and they'd had so much fun. Then Lashelle remembered something she'd been trying to forget. She saw Ken pushing her to have sex, and she experienced her internal conflict as if it were happening in the present. In the dream she saw herself giving in. She woke up sobbing, finally aware of the pattern that had been established that night in the back seat of an old Lincoln.

When Ken wanted her sexually, she hadn't asked herself what she wanted. Out of fear of losing the "big man on campus," she had given in. She had carried the shame of her personal betrayal all these years and blamed Ken for it. Their present sexual pattern had been established thirty-seven years ago. Ken would push, she would give in and abandon herself, and then she would resent him and view him as the enemy.

Ken stirred when Lashelle got out of bed to get a tissue from the bathroom. When she crawled back into bed, he became aware that she

> It is human to make a mistake. There is something wrong if we can't admit it.

Heart2Heart

What is your natural response when your LifeMate hurts you or lets you down? How did you learn to react in this way?

Lashelle denied the hurt that had happened while she and Ken were dating. She had pushed it out of her consciousness and didn't understand its impact on their relationship even after thirty-seven years. In your life, have you experienced an injury that you didn't acknowledge as important until much later? Explain.

What has been your most personally meaningful experience of asking for or receiving forgiveness?

was crying. He held her and asked her what was wrong. The story poured out. Both of them cried. Ken expressed his remorse for his actions. Lashelle wept as she talked about abandoning herself in order to please him. They hugged each other until the sun came up. A new day was dawning in their marriage.

From Dave's Journal:

About six years into our marriage, I built our home in Canada. We were operating on a very tight budget. When it came to finishing the house the way we wanted, I realized we had exhausted our resources. Instead of disappointing Jan, I overextended our budget to get some things we both wanted. In doing so, I put myself under considerable stress. Jan kept asking me what was wrong, and I would sidestep the issue. Eventually she found out the truth. I had overspent, and I had withheld that truth from her. I had to ask Jan's forgiveness for withholding the truth from her and treating her like a child who couldn't handle the reality of our finances. My way to avoid potential conflict with Jan was to withhold the truth. I did not want to face her disappointment and the probable conflict that would follow.

From Jan's Journal:

When I discovered the truth, I was doubly angry. I was angry because Dave had sidestepped my inquiries, and I was angry that I hadn't been included in the financial decision. Before I understood Dave's perspective, I assumed that Dave had not told me in order to protect his ego and to maintain the upper hand. After I dared to listen to why he had done this, I understood his hesitancy. I had to admit that in the past I had made him pay for disappointing me.

I blamed him, withdrew from him, criticized him, became quite con-demning, and chose to make him miserable. I would act, in those early years, as if his job was to please me. Well, needless to say there was no scriptural justification for either my attitude or my actions. I had to shift from my self-righteous perspective that Dave was the "problem" in our marriage. I needed to change my attitude and my way of responding in a time of conflict. I needed to ask David to also forgive me.

Being married doesn't mean that we always feel loving. It means we never cease to care. When we are hurt we feel pain. It is natural not to feel affectionate at those moments, but it is not okay to cease caring and to abandon the struggle.

Read the following list of myths about forgiveness. Put a checkmark by the statements you identify with.

In the past I have believed that forgiving my LifeMate makes it necessary for me to:

Him Her

____ ____ Pretend that the injury didn't happen. "I wasn't hurt."

____ ____ Ignore the pain. "What pain?"

____ ____ Minimize the pain. "It's no big deal."

____ ____ Forget the pain. "If I forgive I should forget."

____ ____ Excuse or condone my LifeMate. "It really wasn't his or her fault."

____ ____ Deny my LifeMate's responsibility. "He or she didn't mean to do it."

____ ____ Give permission to continue the behavior. "Men will be men."

____ ____ Forgive even while the injury is continuing. This kind of forgiveness is like absolving a debt that was paid off with a bad check.

Heart2Heart

Where did you get your model of forgiveness? Explain. Have one of these myths been true in your style of forgiveness? Give an example.

Explain what happened to your spirit as a result of acting on one of these myths. How did it impact your LifeMate?

The Response to Conviction

God has never looked for perfect people. He only looks for faithful ones. The Bible is full of stories of people who fell flat on their faces over and over and over again. We are all broken. "There is no one who does good, not even one"(Ps. 14:3). Hebrews 11 lists the Scriptural Hall of Fame. In it we read of men and women who even though they failed are held up as models for us to emulate. Why? Because when they failed, they admitted it, they reconnected to God and to his people, and moved forward in faith.

Have you ever felt an internal warning light go off before you are going to let your LifeMate have a piece of your mind? You ignore the warning and then either bombard your LifeMate with harsh words or roll your eyes, sigh and let him or her know without saying a word that you think your spouse is an idiot.

Usually it isn't too long before you are convicted by the Holy Spirit. How do you respond? Does your angry condemning conscience take over? Do you feel shame and guilt?

It's been said that guilt is the gift that keeps on giving. As a result of guilt we all develop a serious condition called in-grown eyeballs. Guilt focuses on what a "schmo" we are. The worse we feel about ourselves, the more we condemn ourselves, and then the more we increase the likelihood that we repeat our hurtful patterns. After numerous guilt attacks, we begin to feel hopelessly flawed and utterly discouraged.

In Romans 8:1 we read Paul's incredibly powerful and reassuring words: "Therefore, there is now no condemnation for those who are in Christ Jesus." He died to eradicate our guilt so that we could face our need for growth rather than wallowing in guilt and shame. Jesus wants to love us into growth. When we hurt our LifeMates the Holy Spirit convicts us, but guilt is not his tool. Nowhere in Scripture do we discover that feeling guilty and bad about ourselves leads to repentance. A guilty Christian is an oxymoron if we study God's Word.[1]

Your Choice: Guilt or Grief!

What, then, leads to repentance? The answer is found in 2 Corinthians 7:10. Godly sorrow (grief) leads to repentance. Godly sorrow's focus is on the person we have just hurt and our damaged relationship. Rather than being self-focused, it is other-focused. There is such a radical difference between feeling sorry that our attitudes or actions have caused someone we love pain or feeling guilty and condemned that we have failed yet another time.

Have you ever been hurt by someone who keeps talking about what a low-life he or she is, rather than acknowledging awareness and sorrow for how his attitude or behavior hurt you? It's a frustrating place to be in. Perhaps you didn't even understand why you were frustrated. You are the one who has been hurt, and now the other person is the victim. Your pain and the damage to your relationship are being ignored. It's all about the other person.

Godly sorrow abandons guilt and moves toward the restoration of the relationship. Guilt leaves us in a spiraling downward self-focused whirlpool of shame. Grief leaves us sad that we have hurt our LifeMate and damaged our marriage. Guilt focuses on our failure and how lousy we feel; grief, in contrast, allows us to put ourselves in our LifeMate's shoes and focus on how he or she feels. Love and empathy take over.

As the recipient of God's amazing love we are to pass on that same love to others. When we fail the Holy Spirit convicts us. The Holy Spirit is about love. The Holy Spirit's conviction comes with an absolute absence of condemnation. What is the purpose of the Holy Spirit's conviction? It is to make us aware of how we are hurting God, our LifeMates or ourselves

> The first lie detector was made out of the rib of a man. And they have been unable to improve on that model ever since!

by our behavior and attitudes. It is to lead us to grieve and repent that we have failed to love. It is to lead us to reconnect with God, the source of all love, and with our LifeMate, the object of our love. As Christians we are to live beyond the law. We are to love!

Rate your ability to hear your LifeMate's pain. It can be difficult to admit that we have hurt our LifeMates' hearts. Yet it is impossible to move to maturity and love if we are unwilling to take responsibility for the pain we have caused someone we love, even if it was not our intention to hurt them. Take the time to answer the following questions honestly using this rating scale:

1	2	3	4	5
Rarely	Seldom	Periodically	Frequently	Always

When your LifeMate tells you that something you did, neglected to do, said, or neglected to say caused him or her pain, do you …

Him Her

_____ _____ Attempt to blame your LifeMate for the situation.

_____ _____ Tell your LifeMate that he or she is "emotional" or "stupid" (insert your favorite word of choice) for feeling that way.

_____ _____ Look for ways to make your LifeMate feel as bad as you are feeling at this moment.

_____ _____ Find ways to punish your LifeMate for having hurt your feelings.

_____ _____ Attempt to make your LifeMate feel guilt or shame for bringing such a thing up to you when he or she is not so perfect either.

If you scored high, when wronged you often have a sense of justice, power, and superiority. Unfortunately, none of these promote your growth either personally or relationally. Often we need to ask ourselves,

"Am I more invested in being right and staying angry, or am I more invested in moving toward love?"

Transition to Becoming a Person of Grace and Truth

A skill that each of us needs to develop is the ability to give and receive a heart-felt apology. Nothing renews love like an effective apology. It alleviates pain, disinfects bad feelings, and promotes healing. How does an apology work this magic?

Effective apologies acknowledge what just happened. They offer regret for the hurt that resulted from the incident. They convey that the hurt wasn't intentional. They move on to repair the hurt.

Many of us think of an apology as a simple matter of saying, "I'm sorry." That is a step in the right direction. When we choose to learn how to effectively apologize, the benefits in our marriage are overwhelming. We are letting our LifeMate know that we truly regret what just happened and our part in it.

The Effective Apology

1. Express regret and accept responsibility. Be specific.

   Jim: I'm sorry that I made that wisecrack about your cooking when we were out with the Smiths."

   Connie: "I'm sorry that I didn't take that package to Federal Express for you today when I promised you I would get to it."

2. Convey non-intentionality if that is true. This was not a premeditated crime. Say explicitly that you didn't mean to cause hurt or harm.

   Jim: "I am embarrassed that the put-down popped out of my mouth. I didn't plan on making you feel small."

Heart2Heart

1. **How much do you think it would improve your relationship with your LifeMate if you took responsibility for the injuries that you inflict? Discuss your answers together.**

2. **Where did you learn to adopt any of the above patterns?**

3. **How would a recent altercation have been different if one or both of you had taken responsibility for the pain you caused?**

Connie: "I certainly didn't mean for my procrastination to put you in an awkward situation."

3. Explain what happened. This isn't an excuse. Describe the circumstances. Put it in context.

Jim: "I got competitive with John. He was firing out some one-liners and I topped him, but at your expense."

Connie: "I got preoccupied with my agenda, and I kept putting off the nagging thought that I needed to drive to the Federal Express office. When I got there, I felt sick. It was past time in order to get your package out that day."

4. Repair the damage.

Jim: "I'm going to phone John and let him know that I really regret my words. I want to be the kind of husband who affirms his wife, not puts her down."

Connie: "I will be at the Federal Express office when they open tomorrow morning. It will be the first thing on my agenda. Are you okay with that?"

Ruth Bell Graham said, "A good marriage is the union of two forgivers."[2] Kissing and making up achieve two purposes in a marriage. We see that petty squabbles are nothing but momentary bumps in the road in an otherwise healthy, loving relationship. The second purpose it achieves is that it reminds us of how much we truly love each other even in the midst of being a little bent out of shape.

Heart2Heart

Think back to a time in the last few weeks when an apology on your part would have helped the situation.

Using the four step Effective Apology model, apologize. Tell your LifeMate what it was like giving and receiving this kind of an apology.

A Scriptural Challenge!

You can pray very simply, like this:

"Our Father in heaven,

Reveal who you are.

Set the world right;

Do what's best—

As above, so below.

Keep us alive with three square meals.

Keep us forgiven with you and forgiving others …

In prayer there is a connection between what God

does and what you do. You can't get forgiveness

from God, for instance, without also forgiving others.

If you refuse to do your part, you cut

yourself off from God's part."

Matthew 6:9, 10, 14, 15 (MSG)

Do an inventory on your patterns of forgiveness. First look at how you forgive your LifeMate. Then look at how you receive forgiveness from your LifeMate.

Put a checkmark by the statements that are true of you. When I move in the direction of forgiving my LifeMate where do I get stuck?

Him Her

_____ _____ I get conflicted. Part of me wants to forgive, but the other part of me wants my LifeMate to hurt like I am.

_____ _____ I naturally go into a one-up, critical, condemning place.

_____ _____ When I am hurt by my LifeMate's actions it is difficult for me to feel any love for my LifeMate.

_____ _____ I want to distance and pull away. It is difficult for me to move toward my LifeMate by initiating loving actions.

_____ _____ It is difficult for me to ask for what I need my LifeMate to do in order to build trust.

Heart2Heart

1. The way we treat each other is the way we treat Jesus. Based on the passage above, what can you assume is God's response when you refuse to apologize or to receive an apology from your LifeMate?

2. In Matthew 5:23–24 what must happen prior to a time of prayer and worship? Who leaves his or her gift at the altar? What does this tell you about God?

3. Which do you find a greater challenge: to tell your LifeMate that you have been hurt, or to offer your LifeMate forgiveness for a hurt he or she caused? Why do you think that is so?

_____ _____ I don't want to believe that my LifeMate's remorse or apology is genuine.

_____ _____ I get afraid of being hurt again and so I distance.

_____ _____ I treat every mistake of my LifeMate's as if it is a ten on a ten-point scale.

_____ _____ I have a difficult time coming alongside my LifeMate as a normal person who made a mistake.

_____ _____ Other_____.

Based on your answers to this inventory, is there something you need to do with your support partner to help you move in the direction of offering forgiveness to your LifeMate? What do you believe your next step needs to be?

In this next step, put a check mark by the statements that are true of you.

When I receive forgiveness from my LifeMate, I find it extremely difficult because:

Him Her

_____ _____ I go straight to shame and guilt rather than godly sorrow that I have hurt my LifeMate's heart.

_____ _____ I place myself in a "one-down" position in my head.

_____ _____ I feel that I am a failure, that I am bad.

_____ _____ I am afraid that my LifeMate will think less of me now.

_____ _____ I think critical thoughts about my LifeMate.

_____ _____ I want to make my LifeMate feel bad too.

_____ _____ I am conflicted. One part of me wants to accept love, but one part of me wants to reject it.

_____ _____ I am afraid that my LifeMate will love me less.

_____ _____ I find it hard to receive my LifeMate's love.

_____ _____ I find it hard to trust that this won't be brought up and used against me in some way in the future.

When Forgiveness Is Complete!

Forgiveness is complete when:

- The unrewarding role of "saint and sinner" has been abandoned.
- You have listened so completely that you can see the situation through your LifeMate's eyes. Empathy is active in your relationship.
- You have spoken clearly about what you need in order to heal.
- Your approach to problems is solution-oriented not blame-oriented.
- You remember the pain without reliving it. The injury is no longer the focus of daily life.
- You have committed never to use this as Exhibit A in an angry interchange.
- You are willing to be influenced by your LifeMate again.
- Conflicts are welcomed and worked through. They do not escalate.
- You present a united front in dealing with others.
- You are reconnecting sexually with love and passion.
- You both maintain solid boundaries with people of the opposite sex and with outside influences that could threaten the marriage.
- You both maintain your own individuality and separateness.
- You are no longer preoccupied with the possibility of relapse.
- You can verbalize the learning that has taken place.
- You are creating new positive memories together.

> To carry a grudge is like being stung to death by one bee.
>
> William H. Walton
>
> (Allen Klein, Winning Words, Portland House, New York 2002 Page 236)

There's a difference between false forgiveness and true forgiveness. If, as a result of a LifeMate's hurtful choice, you choose to live in any of these ways, then you have not forgiven your LifeMate:

I live **OVER** you—in a state of self-righteous superiority. I control. You are the sinner and I am the saint.

I live **IN SPITE OF** you—I am indifferent to your pain. I ignore you. I do my own thing.

I live **AGAINST** you—I make you the enemy. I punish you.

I live **WITHOUT** you—I isolate and pull away from you.

I live **FOR** you—I take responsibility for your choice. It must be my fault that you did this.

If you can make these choices, then you have forgiven:

I live **WITH** you—I love you and level with you.

I care for you and I confront you.

I speak my truth as I offer you grace.

Heart**2**Heart

Rate yourself on the scale at right in reference to your level of connection. Where do you see yourself on this continuum? Share with your LifeMate.

Red Zone	Yellow Zone	Green Zone
I hold grudges when my Life-Mate hurts me. I go into a place of guilt and self-condemnation when I fail.	I want to avoid the problem and my LifeMate. I am conflicted. Sometimes I feel guilty. Sometimes I grieve.	I offer and ask for forgiveness. I grieve that I have damaged our love. I move toward repair.

Week 1: Pillow Talk

1. Can you remember a time from your childhood when an adult gave you an apology? What kind of impact did that have on you?

2. If you never had that experience, what kind of impact did that have on you?

Week 2: Pillow Talk

1. Has there been a time in your marriage when your LifeMate helped you understand grace (unmerited favor)? What was that like for you?

2. Think of the people who are important to you. Who would you say has been a supportive, forgiving, available fellow struggler? Give examples. What has this person's friendship meant to you?

Week 3: Pillow Talk

1. What does it mean to you personally to have a relationship with a God who convicts of sin but doesn't condemn you?
2. What makes you feel guilty?
3. Talk about a time when your feelings of guilt turned your focus away from love and onto what a "schmo" you were. How did that affect your relationship?

Week 4: Pillow Talk

1. What part does confession—saying "I am sorry"—play in your personal life?
2. How would you like confession to be a part of your marital relationship? Some couples come together at the end of the day to pray together. At that time, they ask each other if there is any hurt blocking their love that needs to be talked through. Some couples come together once a week and ask a similar question. Some just do it as the need arises.

FROM PREVIOUS MONTH:
I COMMIT TO MAKE INTENTIONAL CHOICES
THAT ENRICH OUR MARRIAGE!

> **IN MY DESIRE TO LIVE ONE GOOD YEAR OF MARRIAGE WITH MY LIFEMATE,**
>
> I COMMIT TO FORGIVE AND TO BE AWARE OF MY NEED FOR FORGIVENESS!

MONTH
FOUR

"Awareness: Leaving Behind Apathy"

"If marriage is your object,
You'd better start loving your subject!"

HOW CAN YOU TELL WHETHER OR NOT a couple is married? Often they don't seem to have much to say to each other anymore. How do you know couples who are dating? They talk nonstop. They look into each other's eyes. They touch. They ask questions. They assume there is more to know. They are aware!

After being married seven years or more, LifeMates have a tendency to carve out their individual worlds. Then, many of us live in our heads a great deal of the time. When aware, we acknowledge that our LifeMates are separate, fascinating human beings. There is always more to discover about each other, always more to learn. Rather than assuming that we can read minds or that we know everything there is to know about our

The paradox of comfortable love is that we stop trying!

LifeMates, awareness asks questions. Then awareness is interested in the reply from this separate person! Awareness takes off dark, dirty, dingy lenses and exchanges them for clear, sparkling lenses. Awareness searches for what is working, what is new, and what is interesting. Don't we all love those who notice us, affirm us, and make us aware that we matter to them? Awareness assumes growth and asks about it. Awareness energizes. Awareness gets specific. Awareness praises. Awareness initiates. Awareness rejuvenates. Awareness turns lifetime lovers into friends. So awareness needs to be cultivated in a healthy marriage.

A Moment of Awareness

Brooke was so excited. Her school was preparing for an "Honor Dad" day, and Brooke loved her dad. An early morning pancake breakfast would be followed by chapel, and then Dad was going to visit her sixth grade class.

A few days before the event, Brooke's teacher handed out a questionnaire about her dad's childhood and preferences. Brooke was to guess how her dad would answer the questions. Here are some sample questions:

What is your favorite ice cream?

When you were in the sixth grade, who was your best friend and why?

What was your favorite sport as a kid?

Did you take lessons of any kind when in sixth grade?

What did you like best about being eleven or twelve?

Brooke took the assignment seriously and thought about her answers. The long anticipated day arrived. Brooke loved bringing her dad to school. He was a fun dad and all her friends liked him too. She felt a sense of pride and excitement as she enjoyed time together with him. It was nice not having to share him with Mom or with her sister for once. Pancakes had never tasted so good, and chapel—well, she felt so loved and important sitting next to her dad. She could hardly wait to see if she had guessed right on the answers to the questionnaire. Sure enough, she'd nailed many of the answers, but she learned there was a lot she didn't know about her dad and his childhood. She listened to her dad's answers with enthusiasm. Both daughter and dad learned a great deal about each other that day.

After school Brooke found her mother and showed her the questionnaire she had completed. When her mother read the questions, she realized that there were many items that she didn't know how to answer. They had been married eigthteen years and yet there was so much more to learn. She had assumed that she knew her husband pretty well, and she did, but obviously she had more research to do.

From Dave's Journal:

Shortly after we were married Jan came back from a shopping trip. She had purchased a new dress for Christmas that she excitedly put on and came out to model for me. She inquired, "Well, what do you think?" I replied in an almost monotone voice, "Looks fine."

WRONG ANSWER, GUYS! I probably was watching a football game when she asked me that question. Anyway, she was not pleased. Since then I have learned, and I have removed "fine" from my vocabulary. The bottom line is I spaced out. I was not really focused and aware. I'm a fast learner. I changed my ways. I have polished my skills over thirty-two years of marriage. I have learned that timing is important. Jan loves it when I notice and comment with gusto about a new hairdo or a new outfit. I blow it in her mind if I need to be prodded. Awareness pays off!

Heart2Heart

1. Share an example from your marriage when you realized that you had put your relationship on automatic pilot. Perhaps you had stopped really seeing each other, greeting each other, or talking to each other.

2. In the beginning of your dating relationship, what was it like to be together?

3. At that time what did you value and appreciate about each other? Despite the challenges of the last few years, do you still see in your LifeMate some of the qualities that you just described?

From Jan's Journal:

Last November our precious daughter, Amy, married Garrett Heath Pendergraft. The entire experience—the months leading up to the wedding, the planning, the parties, welcoming and embracing a new family, and the wedding itself—turned out to be one of the most joyous experiences that Dave and I have ever shared. On the day of the wedding everywhere we looked there were people we treasured and loved.

As I watched Amy and Garrett, I remembered that fabulous time in our life—the engagement period. It was an amazing stage. We were both on a perpetual high. We felt loved. Dave was crazy about me, and he liked my quirks. I felt the same way about him. It was as if every interaction was electric and charged. We couldn't stand to be apart. We couldn't wait to be together. We loved being loved. Marriage had to teach us how to love.

There have been times in our marriage where catching a glimpse of couples who seem close, tender, and interested set off feelings of sadness in me. Perhaps I'd watch an older couple talking and sharing with each other enthusiastically over their meal while we didn't seem to have anything to talk about except our children or our work. At other times I'd watch a couple being affectionate, or I'd overhear them bragging about each other. That made me aware of how mundane our relationship had become. We ran an effective business, but it seemed to me that we'd lost touch with each other. I think we both felt unnoticed at home except for our roles as mother and wife or father and husband. It seemed like we had lost sight of each other.

Given my natural inclination I wanted to blame this sad state of affairs on David, but it seems after thirty-two years of marriage, I am no longer comfortable with that analysis. If I am feeling bored, I have probably become boring. If I'm feeling unappreciated, I have to ask myself,

When attempting to change old habits, it is normal to have lapses. Don't allow them to become relapses!

"When was the last time I appreciated and admired Dave?" If I'm feeling envious, what is it I'm wishing we had? Can I initiate that in our own relationship? If I'm feeling like there is nothing left to know, can I ask questions?

Transition Toward Awareness

"I can change how I see you. Although my thoughts are conflicted with demands, my feelings are confused with mixed emotions, my intentions are ambivalent in divided directions, I can redefine how I see you. Often this is the only change possible as a beginning point."[1]

Take a few minutes to jot down on separate paper what you know about the following topics in relation to your LifeMate. Then check with your LifeMate to see if you are aware of your LifeMate's world.

Friends:

Recent Important Events:

Upcoming Anticipated Events:

Current Stresses:

Hopes and Dreams:

How did you do on this quick awareness check?

The rest of this chapter is a series of Heart 2 Heart activities that will help you continue to build awareness about your LifeMate's world. Complete as many as you can together.

Heart2Heart

1. Do you believe that your major challenge in the awareness area comes from your attitudes, your thoughts, your feelings, or your habits? Explain.

2. What will prevent you from being aware once you are finished with this chapter?

3. How do you think increased awareness would contribute to the quality of your marriage?

Heart2Heart

How aware are you of basic information? If you don't know the answers to these questions about your LifeMate, find out now!

Marriage Insurance Information

My LifeMate's birthday:

Our anniversary:

My LifeMate's

dress size:

Slacks or pant size:

Jeans size:

Shirt or blouse size:

Underwear size:

Shoe size:

Ring size:

My LifeMate's favorite:

Color:

Movie:

Perfume/Cologne:

Play:

Author:

Musical:

Singer:

Sport:

Magazine:

Jewelry: gold, silver, platinum

Candy:

Hobby:

Cookie:

Meal/dessert:

Restaurant:

Vacation spot:

Warning! Once you have completed the above marriage insurance form, you can never again plead ignorance. Isn't that great?

Heart2Heart

Of all the possessions that your LifeMate owns, select one that is very important at this point in his or her life. If you were forced to flee your home with only three items, this would be one of the items your LifeMate would take. Both of you bring the object or a picture of it to the kitchen table if possible.

1. Why did you choose this object, and why do you believe it is so important to your LifeMate?

2. What does this object say about your LifeMate? Do you believe your LifeMate will view it as important five years from now?

3. How do you each feel about the way your LifeMate sees you as demonstrated by the selection of your prized possession? What item would you have chosen for yourself? Why?

Heart2Heart

Complete the following questionnaire by answering true or false to each of the following statements. Discuss these with your LifeMate.

Him   Her

____ ____   My LifeMate greets me after he or she has been away from me.

____ ____   My LifeMate welcomes me after I have been away from him/her.

____ ____   I don't often feel ignored.

____ ____   My LifeMate gives me eye contact when talking to me.

____ ____   My LifeMate seeks out my opinions.

____ ____   My LifeMate touches me a lot.

____ ____   I believe that what I say is important to my LifeMate.

____ ____   My LifeMate is genuinely interested in my world.

____ ____   My LifeMate expresses gratitude for actions I do for him/her.

_____ _____ My LifeMate includes me in his/her life.

_____ _____ My LifeMate tells me that I am attractive.

_____ _____ My LifeMate is a good friend.

_____ _____ My LifeMate welcomes me into his/her world.

_____ _____ My LifeMate enjoys spending time with me.

_____ _____ My LifeMate expresses affection toward me.

_____ _____ My LifeMate loves me.

_____ _____ My LifeMate comments on details of my appearance that let me know I am noticed.

What have you learned from this experience?

Heart 2 Heart

Directions: Listed below are questions designed to facilitate discovery of each other. Over the coming months take a couple of these questions with you on a date night or share your responses over a cup of coffee. Have fun growing in your awareness of each other. Don't feel pressured to answer all these questions this month.

If you could stay one age for your entire life, which would you choose? Why?

If money was not the issue, what would you choose for your profession?

What book has had the most effect on you? In what way did it impact you?

If you could live anywhere in the world for one year and not have to work, where would you want to go? Why?

What was your favorite subject in school? Do you use that in your job today?

What is your favorite holiday? What do you most like about it?

What is one thing in life you haven't done that you regret not doing?

What three qualities do you require in a friendship?

If you had to spend three months alone on an island, what possessions, besides those essential for survival, would you want to have with you? Why?

If you were casting a film about your life, who would play the main characters in it? Why?

What is the best piece of advice that a friend ever gave you?

What is a newspaper headline that you would like to read about yourself?

What is a lesson in life you learned the hard way?

Have you had one dream more than once? What is it? What do you believe is its significance?

Talk about your greatest fear about aging.

What is a piece of music that has had a profound effect on you? What is it about that music that touches your heart?

What do you consider your most attractive physical feature? Why do you like it?

If you could visit any time period, which one would you choose and why? The Roman Empire, Classical Greece, Victorian England, King Arthur's Court, the 60s, the Wild West, Colonial America, the Roaring Twenties, the Stone Age?

What do you wish you had started to learn as a kid? What keeps you from learning it now?

Would you rather be married to a famous person or be famous yourself? Why?

What do you enjoy doing and even consider fun that most other people regard as hard work?

If you had an extra day every month that no one else had, what are the ways you would spend it?

What is the best complement you could receive about your work?

What are the best and worst aspects of your job?

If you could do it over, what event or thing would you change in your life?

What three things stress you out on a regular basis?

What is the most interesting question that anyone ever asked you?

Heart**2**Heart

Practice your art of observation for seven days in a row. Look at your life through the eyes of an artist. Each day share two new observations with your LifeMate: one observation having to do with your external surroundings, and one observation having to do with your LifeMate—how he or she looks, how he or she relates, something you value about who your LifeMate is. Try to comment on things that you don't usually notice or discuss. For example:

External:

- Fascinating architecture that catches your eye
- Unusual food items carried in a local store
- Plants, flowers, trees that you particularly like
- Your favorite time of day and why

LifeMate:

- A favorite expression of your LifeMate
- A tender moment that your LifeMate shared with one of your children
- Some emotion that you thought you saw in your LifeMate's eyes
- A moment of empathy shared that felt wonderful
- An outfit that made your LifeMate look smashing
- A physical feature of your LifeMate that you enjoy

Red Zone	Yellow Zone	Green Zone
I have my head in the sand most of the time.	I struggle with thinking my Life-Mate is like me. Periodically I value him as a separate person.	I value my Life-Mate as a separate, growing person. I check my awareness on a daily basis.

Rate yourself on the scale at left in reference to your level of connection. Where do you see yourself on this continuum? Share with your LifeMate.

Week 1: Date Night

Go through each of your family photo albums or baby books. Reminisce. Enjoy the stories. Then enjoy photographs from your married life together. Bring your favorite snack to share with your LifeMate.

Week 2: Date Night

Have a double feature movie night. Rent and watch each other's favorite movie. Don't forget the popcorn.

Week 3: Date Night

One LifeMate plans an adventure for the two of you. It needs to be something that the planner really likes to do. It should happen at the planner's favorite time of day and include the planner's favorite food. Keep it a surprise. Specify attire. The other LifeMate is to show up with enthusiasm to enjoy what his or her LifeMate has planned. If you need a sitter, the planner finds one.

Week 4: Date Night

The other LifeMate plans an adventure for the two of you around the interests, cuisine of choice, and favorite time of day of this LifeMate. Keep it a surprise! The planner from last week is to show up with enthusiasm to enjoy anything his or her LifeMate has planned. If you need a sitter, the planner finds one.

FROM PREVIOUS MONTH:

I COMMIT TO FORGIVE AND TO BE AWARE
OF MY NEED FOR FORGIVENESS.

IN MY DESIRE TO LIVE ONE GOOD YEAR
OF MARRIAGE WITH MY LIFEMATE,

I COMMIT TO PRACTICE AWARENESS OF MY
LIFEMATE ON AN ONGOING BASIS.

M O N T H
FIVE

"Boundaries: Leaving Behind Indifference"

> *"You've got to think about 'big things' while you're doing small things, so that all the small things go in the right direction."*

Alvin Toffler[1]

DO BOUNDARIES KEEP US IN OR OUT?

LifeMates who are boundary lovers choose to make their relationship primary by constructing a protective wall around it. The boundary protects their love from anyone or anything—good or bad—that could pull them apart. It keeps forces that have the power to divide them outside their relationship. Together LifeMates deal with the world outside their boundaries through a shared window of openness and honesty. They make certain that there is a wall around their marriage but that there are no walls between the two of them. In that environment of honesty, openness, freedom, responsibility, and safety, love thrives! Boundaries in marriage are fundamentally about love.

A Couple Without Boundaries

Although Phyllis and George had been married twenty-seven years, it seemed to them that marriage was getting tougher rather than easier.

Never forget that any relationship can fall apart.

George traveled a lot with his work. He was a brilliant entrepreneur who conducted a great deal of business in the Far East. It was often necessary for him to be in Hong Kong for a month at a time.

When he wasn't traveling, his office was in their home. That meant Phyllis saw him all the time or she didn't see him at all. This left her often feeling off balance.

Phyllis had been a stay-at-home mom since the boys were young, but now that they were older, she filled the void with Bible studies and volunteer work. Six years ago, she had been diagnosed with breast cancer. Now she was an active and appreciated volunteer for the American Cancer Society.

Last year they moved George's mother from her home into a care facility. Mom was not pleased with the move. On a daily basis she would phone asking George and Phyllis to bring her things. When George was home he would visit his mother regularly. He would ask her what she needed, but it seemed she rarely remembered until he had arrived back home.

In the process of the move, George discovered that his mother's finances were in a disorganized state. Phyllis had a background in accounting, so she attempted to create order out of chaos. At one point George's mother accused Phyllis of stealing from her. George was out of town at the time, which seemed to be the pattern whenever there was a problem. Frankly, George got tired of dealing with the problems. He hated confronting his mother. He'd either lose it and rage or withdraw in an angry silence.

The only way that Mom could go to church or to her multiple medical appointments was if Phyllis or George took her. Faithfully every Sunday they picked her up and took her out to lunch after church. When George was out of town, Phyllis assumed these responsibilities by herself.

At lunch Mom complained about the care facility and her financial situation—or she would say nothing. It was hardly an uplifting experience.

As if Mom didn't complicate their life enough, their youngest son Stan had moved back home to live with them. He was a musician and an artist who was having a terrible time finding a job. He'd had some good jobs, but he always left them for one reason or another. Stan had battled with alcoholism since his early teens. He was not in recovery.

It was not unusual for Phyllis to return home from an afternoon meeting to find her home overtaken by young people. The music was blaring and there would be beer bottles and snacks all over the budding musician's space. Phyllis would find herself getting tense as she got close to home. She threatened George that either their son or she was going to leave. She begged George to do something. He just retreated further and further into his shell. He used work as an escape. Yet when Stan wanted money or the use of the car, George accommodated him. On the rare occasion that George didn't come through, Stan knew he could always go to Grandma for a handout. Phyllis didn't know what to do anymore. She felt alone and undermined.

Phyllis and George were becoming more and more estranged. Phyllis was becoming more and more depressed. Stan was becoming more and more dependent. He would party all night and sleep until noon. Phyllis would lie awake all night upset and anxious. George was taking sleeping pills. What were they to do?

A wise woman who was gaining a daughter-in-law told her son that wives always come before mothers. It's no surprise her daughter-in-law and she became good friends!

From Jan's Journal:

In my work as a therapist, I have witnessed the immense pain caused by intrusive parents in their adult child's marriage. In fact, when I have the privilege of doing premarital counseling, I send a questionnaire to the

Heart2Heart

1. What intruders had invaded Phyllis and George's life? In what areas had they not set boundaries? How had their team become divided?

2. What are the intruders that challenge your marriage?

3. Are there ways that you have let these intruders pull the two of you apart? Explain.

parents and stepparents on both sides. By answering questions, parents put their expectations down on paper. For example, two of the questions are: "How often do you expect to see or talk with this couple in a week? How involved in your celebration of the major holidays do you expect these young people to be?" Let me tell you, I've watched sparks fly as couples come face to face with parental expectations.

Well, now, suddenly it seems I'm the parent and mother-in-law. Now I know how it feels when my daughter phones and excitedly talks about the Thanksgiving celebration she and Garrett are planning in Cordova, Tennessee with Marsi and Philip. I love Marsi and Philip. I actively encourage Amy and Garrett's trips to his home. I'm thrilled that Amy has married into such an incredible family, and yet I'm still a mom. There is no couple I'd rather have at our Thanksgiving table than this precious one.

Boundaries have kept me from picking up the phone and talking to Amy when I know Garrett is home. They have resulted in my hearing their boundary, "No, Mom, not tonight, we have made other plans" or "Mom, we can drop by for two hours and then we're going out with some friends," without laying a guilt trip on them. Boundaries mean that I don't just drop in to Amy and Garrett's home when I get the urge. At the beginning, in some ways honoring their boundaries made me feel like I just couldn't be myself. Celebrating their boundaries meant I had to grieve the reality that I couldn't always have it the way I would choose. Hearing their boundaries sometimes makes me sad and always makes me grow up.

Transition Toward Boundaries

Imagine going to a pet store and buying a dog. You take it home, put it in the backyard, and then ignore it from that point on. The dog gets no food, no water, no shots, no love, and no exercise. What kind of a person would you be? Yet many of us treat our marriages that same way. It is all too easy to neglect, ignore, and abandon our relationships and our LifeMates.

We become addicted to the adrenaline rush that is the result of a harried life. Some of us don't feel important unless we are harried. We forget that life is not supposed to run us, we are to run it. So often, we let the good things in life get in the way of the best. Forsaking all others to make marriage top priority may mean that we don't waste energy pursuing things or spending time with people who don't support the high value we give marriage. At the same time, we don't give up anything that supports our relationship.

An important task of marriage is learning when to say yes and when to say no. We need to ask ourselves the following question: "If I say yes to this request, will it strengthen our marriage, and will I stay true to my value system?" On a daily basis we need to renew our wedding vows. In every choice we make we need to consider our marriage. We need to stay true to the values that support our identity, and we need to verbalize and demonstrate our LifeMate's importance in our lives. A married couple is not two singles sharing a household; they are two people, but they have a united life. They consider each other in everything they do.

Setting Boundaries with Parents

The theme of leaving parents to be joined to a LifeMate is repeated five times in Scripture. Mark wrote about this theme.

"In the original creation, God made male and female to be together. Because of this, a man leaves father and mother, and in marriage becomes one flesh ... Because God created this organic union of the two sexes, no one should desecrate his art by cutting them apart" (Mark 10: 6–9 MSG).

Incredible pain results when one LifeMate continues to allow or to

Heart2Heart

Heart to Heart:

1. Check the following challenges you both face most often with parents and parents-in-law.

_____ They visit too often.

_____ They stay too long when they come over.

_____ They phone either too little or too often.

_____ Rather than coming over, they take over.

_____ They expect to be waited on and rarely lift a finger.

_____ They try to tell us how to do life/marriage/parenting, and so forth.

_____ They do not keep our confidences even when asked to.

_____ They are critical of me or my LifeMate.

_____ They try to get us embroiled in the middle of their problems.

_____ They buy things that only one of us wants.

_____ Other

2. What characteristics in your parents and in your parents-in-law do you most value? Write them down. When there really isn't a workable solution in some extended family conflicts, focus on these valuable characteristics.

3. If you say "NO" to either of your parents, what is their reaction?

foster parental intrusion in the marriage. "Leaving" is more than geographical; it involves breaking dependence on your parents and establishing a clear boundary around your marital unit.

At different stages in marriage, we need to reevaluate our boundary-setting with parents. Often when a LifeMate is dealing with an aging parent, the LifeMate is less available physically and emotionally to his or her mate. There is a toll of time, energy, finances, and emotions. Often at the same time one or both LifeMates may be struggling with feelings of mortality, anger, helplessness, and a sense of incredibly deep loss. There will be times you will grin together with the tenderness of it all, times you will weep together, times your

LifeMate may want to be left alone. The challenge we all face is how, as our parents become increasingly dependent in their later years, do we maintain our boundaries and still treat our parents with honor?

Remember, as an adult you are the emotional peer of your parents, your siblings, and other extended family members.

Setting Boundaries with Children

Get out of your parenting roles regularly in order to recharge your batteries! When we give to our LifeMates, we are giving to our children. There is no better way to teach love than to model it. When the marriage relationship has priority over parenting roles, we are happier, we have an intimate connection that supports and nurtures each of us, and we are better parents.

It's useless to say, "I'll spend time with my LifeMate only if there is time." We never seem to find the time unless we take the time. Once children enter the picture, so many of our marital interactions are about chores and responsibilities rather than about friendship, intimacy, and fun.

Jeremy and Melinda were cleaning the kitchen together one evening. Melinda was rinsing off the dishes with her back to Jeremy. Suddenly Jeremy asked, "Do you want to go out?" "Oh yes," replied Melinda, who immediately dropped what she was doing, phoned the neighbor girl to take care of the kids, and grabbed her coat. They went out for coffee and had a wonderful time of connection.

The next day Jeremy was telling his buddy at the office about their evening. He said, "It wasn't my wife I asked to go out, it was our family dog!" Both men laughed, but both men also learned. The best thing we can do for our children is to make our marriages a priority.

In a "Dear Abby" column, a woman who had made her new baby a priority above her husband, passed on the following story:

"With the counselor's help, I realized I had blamed my husband for everything that went wrong and didn't recognize the degree to which I was neglecting him. I had forgotten that Carl needed time with me as much as the baby did, and I had put my job as mother ahead of everything—even our marriage. In my desire to be a good mother, I had

Heart2Heart

1. Do you believe that having children had any kind of negative effect on your marriage? Explain.

2. Do your children honor your privacy? Would you like to make changes so that they would? What might those changes be?

3. Does one of you join forces with the children against the other? If so, how could you change that pattern?

become a bad wife and made Carl feel he was inadequate for not caring for the baby exactly the way I would have—not changing enough diapers and not appreciating me.

I was so focused on our baby, I lost sight of the fact that I had changed as much as I had accused my poor husband of changing."

Choose not to over-schedule activities for your children and under-schedule activities for each other. Make time to be lovers instead of just parents.

Setting Boundaries with Work

Your marriage is the most important work you will ever do! The rewards for not setting boundaries around work are incredibly tempting. We are offered money, promotions, approval, titles, and sometimes exotic vacations that we couldn't justify if we didn't win them. There is a great personal satisfaction in a job well done. There is a rush that comes when we are part of a team working long hours to accomplish a task together. Many of us define our very identity on the basis of our work and our career. Ask any person who has been forced to take an early retirement about the emotional consequences of facing that reality. Work provides a platform for creativity. The frustrating situations we encounter at work test and often strengthen our character. Work has an important place in our life. How does work affect your marriage? Make a life, not just a living!

Setting Boundaries with Friends

There is no such thing as an unshakable, untouchable affair-resistant love. Being in love doesn't protect any of us from lust or from much else, as a matter of fact. Periodically it is wise to examine the protective fence that we have built around our relationship. Is it in place? If it is, there will be no wall between us and our LifeMates. Together we will deal openly and honestly with the world outside our boundaries.

Periodically, as a couple, discuss this question: "How much time and energy can we give to our friends without violating the priority that we have assigned to our marriage?

Do you feel obligated to a friend or two who seem to be in a constant crisis mode? If so, when your LifeMate complains, do you see it as control? Explain.

Do you feel closer to your friends than you do your LifeMate? If so, why? Do you share things with your friends that you would never tell your LifeMate?

Setting Boundaries with the Opposite Sex

Any relationship that we have with someone, including our LifeMates, will sooner or later involve some disillusionment. When we take that dissatisfaction to someone of the opposite sex, we are playing with fire.

Infidelity involves any emotional or sexual intimacy that violates trust. When we open a window of intimacy with someone other than our LifeMates, an interior wall of secrecy is erected between us.

Many people who have had affairs are in a state of shock because they never thought it could happen to them. Yet when we, for whatever reason, stop giving the admiration, recognition, and emotional support that nourishes love, and instead begin to confide in someone of the opposite sex, we are heading down a slippery slope.

Since opportunities for unfaithfulness are all around us, what seems to make the difference between LifeMates who succumb and those who

Heart2Heart

1. When you are home at night or on vacations, do you have leftover work projects that need to be completed? Do you have any other options that you might implement so that your work does not interfere with family time?

2. Do you feel more rewarded by work than by marriage and family life? Explain.

3. Do you break dates with your LifeMate or miss family events because of work? How could you make it up to your family when that happens and you have no control over it?

resist? We are all vulnerable if we have a high level of unmet needs in our relationship, and if, at the same time, we have an active fantasy life. This is where communication, even if uncomfortable, between LifeMates is so crucial. Most often what is put into words, is not put into actions. Share your personal vulnerability with each other. Listen and take this communication very seriously. Make the necessary changes in your relationship.

Besides opportunity and vulnerability there are two other factors that determine whether we will succumb or resist temptation. One is commitment to the marriage, and the other is the strength of personal value systems.

A very courageous LifeMate was on the ski slopes with her family when she ran into her first love. He looked fabulous! His hair was silver gray, and in her eyes he'd only become more handsome with age. She barely remembered their interaction because her heart was beating so loudly. He did tell her that his wife had passed away six months before.

It was difficult for her to get him off of her mind for the rest of the family ski vacation. She didn't see him again, but when she got home there was her first love's voice on their answering machine asking if she would meet him for lunch. Once again she became aware of how fast her heart was beating and how flattered she was that he had gone out of his way to get her number.

When she went to her husband to talk about meeting her old flame for lunch, she became aware that she couldn't maintain eye contact with her husband for fear that he would see her excitement at the anticipation of meeting this guy. At that point she caught herself. She confessed to her husband about how obsessed she was with her first love and how just seeing him made her feel young again. Former feelings had been ignited, and her heart was

Heart2Heart

1. Answer "yes" or "no" to these questions and then discuss them together.

2. Are you having more fun with friends than you are having with each other at this time in your life? Explain. Was there a time when it was different?

3. Do you use your friends to get away from your marriage and your family? When?

4. Do you invest more time and energy in your friendships than you do in your marriage? Explain.

pounding when in his presence or even at the sound of his voice.

Her husband pulled her close to himself. He ran his fingers through her hair and then tipped her face toward him. "Honey," he said, "I'm so sorry I can't do that for you anymore!" She nestled into her husband's embrace. Then she phoned her old flame and declined lunch.

Boundaries with an Ex-Spouse

Perhaps you have stood weak-kneed behind a table in a courtroom. The judge's heavy wooden gavel punctuated the finality of the divorce. You may have thought, "It's over. Now I can get on with my life without him or her." Since then you no doubt have come to realize that even though your ties as a couple were legally severed that day, if children were involved, you two will always be a family. There will be school events, soccer games, piano recitals, award ceremonies, holiday celebrations, graduations, and even weddings, not to mention grandchildren. Life at times feels like a fight waiting to happen.

Then your remarriage brought even more challenging dynamics to the already crowded table. Is your relationship with your ex-spouse intruding in your new marriage in a negative way?

Heart2Heart

Answer "yes" or "no" to the following questions. Then discuss whether you need to tighten up the boundaries around your relationship.

1. Do you discuss your dissatisfaction with your mate or your marriage with anyone who could be a potential alternative to your LifeMate?

2. At the first sign of sexual tension or excitement with someone of the opposite sex, do you tell your LifeMate?

3. If your LifeMate expresses concern about your relationship with someone of the opposite sex, do you take that concern seriously?

4. When a friend of the opposite sex wants to share the problems he or she is having in his or her marriage, do you include your LifeMate in the helping gestures?

5. Do you use your computer to mentally betray your LifeMate?

If your answer to #5 is "yes," seek professional help as soon as possible.

Heart2Heart

1. Are you at your ex-spouse's beck and call even when your LifeMate expresses distress over the situation? Is there any way this needs to change? How could it?

2. Do the two of you facilitate your children's relationship with their other parent? How?

3. Can you empathize with the difficult task of your stepchildren having to accept you? How do you reach out to them even if they don't reach back?

Boundaries with Ministry and Community Involvement

We all want to be part of something bigger than ourselves. We want to contribute. We want to believe that our life on planet earth makes a difference. It is crucial to our identity that we operate out of a sense of purpose. Nevertheless, even great things can rob us of the best. Is your quest to make a difference robbing your LifeMate and your family of quality time? Or do you minister out of fullness because you are refreshed as a result of significant couple and family time?

Prior to our wedding, Dr. Gary Collins gave David some valuable advice. His words were, "You have been called to the ministry, David. Never forget that your wife and family are part of your flock! Do not feel guilty about making them a priority."

Boundaries with Addictions

Addictions are covert and sly and seem to sneak into a person's life through the back door. An addict fundamentally believes that he or she is inadequate. Therefore, addicts need something outside of themselves in order to feel whole. They search for the next drink, the next drug, the next relationship, the next meal. If you are married to someone who suffers from an addiction, you know that you don't have your LifeMate's heart—his or her chosen addiction does.

Setting Boundaries with Hobbies, Sports, TV, and Computers

Hobbies, sports, TV, and computers are all great things created to enrich our lives. Playing a game of beach volleyball with some buddies may result in a happy, tanned, and excited LifeMate coming back enthusiastically to spend time with his wife and family. A day dedicated to scrapbooking may result in a happy, satisfied, and inspired LifeMate coming home to make even more memories with her husband. Separateness, well spent, can enrich togetherness. When both LifeMates value and encourage each other's separate interests and don't do anything in their separateness that threatens their togetherness, separateness builds a marriage.

On the other hand, an obsession with hobbies, sports, television, and the computer sabotages the quality of a relationship. Often the LifeMate, delegated to second place, feels angry, frustrated, resentful, confused, and alienated. This LifeMate wonders why the other would rush home to spend time tuning in to a hobby, sport, TV, or the computer and tuning out the people, events, and drama in his or her marriage and family.

LifeMates of sports fanatics watch with fascination as their LifeMates are intently focused, emotionally expressive, utterly involved, totally alive, deeply caring, wildly passionate, and displaying every other sign of rich and rewarding intimate relationships—but not with them. A common joke recycled now and then goes like this: "You love football more than you love me!"

"Yeah, I do, but I love you more than I love basketball." We laugh and ignore the reality of our obsessions. Are your obsessions hurting your love life?

Heart 2 Heart

Answer these questions "yes" or "no" and then discuss the questions together.

1. Do you get more validation from your ministry and community involvement than from your LifeMate? Explain. Share a time recently when your LifeMate's validation really made an impact.

2. Are you capable of saying no when asked to volunteer? When was the last time you turned someone down and were content with your decision?

3. Is your LifeMate upset about the amount of time you give to ministry or community activities? What was the last conflict you had over this topic?

Heart2Heart

Are you an addict? Answer "yes" or "no" to the following questions.

1. Do you feel more self-confident as a result of using?

2. Do you sneak and lie about your habit?

3. Do you use money already budgeted for something else to feed your habit?

4. Have you tried to quit and been unsuccessful?

5. Is it a source of discord in your marriage with your LifeMate?

6. Do you continue even though it creates financial difficulties, work, school, and family problems?

7. Have you ever suffered any legal consequences?

If you answered yes to the majority of these questions you have a severe addiction. Please get help.

If your LifeMate answered yes to the majority of these questions and refuses to get help, get it yourself. You need to make changes even if your LifeMate does not. Do not depend on your LifeMate to grow up before you do!

Rate yourself on the scale at right in reference to your boundary setting. Where do you see yourself on this continuum? Share with your LifeMate.

How many total hours per week do you spend playing, watching, listening, reading about, and talking about your hobbies, sports, or TV programs? How many hours do you spend on the computer? What is your LifeMate doing while you are engaged in these hobbies? More importantly, does your LifeMate complain about the amount of time that these activities take from your together time?

Another measurement whether you need to reconsider these boundaries is how much money you spend per year on hobbies, sports, TV, and the computer. Do you believe that one or all these four items has negatively affected your marriage?

Week 1: Date Night

Meet each other at a romantic restaurant. Arrive in separate cars. Get all dressed up. When you see each other pretend that it's been a long time since you've been together. Both of you bring something interesting to talk about. Off-limit discussion

Red Zone	Yellow Zone	Green Zone
What boundaries? Everyone and every thing else comes first.	We have worked on protecting our relationship against some intruders. We still have work to do.	Our marriage gets top billing. I protect the boundaries around it on a daily basis.

topics are work, children, parents, friends, ministry, community involvement, hobbies, and sports.

Week 2: Pillow talk

1. If you are going to plan a family vacation that would give you family time and also couple time, what might you like to do and what destination might you choose?

   Idea: Family Camp

   Bring along an adolescent or a parent to baby-sit

   Hotels or cruises that provide activities for children and adolescents.

   Bring a friend for your child or teenager.

2. What do you think it would cost? Is this something you would like to do? If so, lay out the steps in the plan. It adds a spirit of adventure to your marriage if you have something to anticipate.

3. In the last year, what was one of the best memories that you made as a couple?

Week 3: Date Night

If your parents or your best friends have been supportive of your marriage, and if they have been careful to encourage but not intrude, write them a thank you note together. If possible, have them over for dinner, give them your card, and let them know how important they are to you and how much you both value their support.

Week 4: Pillow Talk

1. In the last month, what intruders have you had to limit in order to protect the boundary around your relationship?

2. How have you accomplished this?

3. What effect has this had on your relationship?

FROM PREVIOUS MONTH:

I COMMIT TO PRACTICE AWARENESS OF MY
LIFEMATE ON AN ONGOING BASIS.

**IN MY DESIRE TO LIVE ONE GOOD YEAR
OF MARRIAGE WITH MY LIFEMATE,**

I COMMIT TO PROTECT THE BOUNDARIES
OF OUR MARRIAGE.

MONTH

SIX

"Connecting: Leaving Behind Distance"

> *"Did I pick the right person? This question inverts the starting and ending points. We do not pick a perfect match because we ourselves are not perfect. The universe hands us a flawless diamond—in the rough. Only if we are willing to polish off every part of ourselves that cannot join do we end up with a soul mate."*[1]

HEALTHY CONNECTORS VALUE THEIR LifeMates' freedom to be different. Connectors cherish their LifeMates' experience of life. They delight in the question, "Who is this fascinating person I married?" Connectors expect two opinions, tastes, and needs to be brought to the marriage. Connectors know that differences inform, enrich, and enliven our lives. They also know that at times those same differences irritate and aggravate. Yet connectors embrace their LifeMates' differences with respect and curiosity because learning often comes as a result of differences. Love grows out of differences, not sameness.

Connectors value precious moments of relatedness that bring a warm memory to each LifeMate. These shared experiences become, over time, an emotional thread that ties their hearts together. Connectors build a reservoir of goodwill through small tasks that are done together, quiet conversations when the day's pressures are set aside, soft words of understanding, encouragement offered in difficult moments, the small unexpected gift that says, "I thought of you today," moments of companionship, and spontaneous acts of service and gestures of love. Healthy connectors warm their LifeMates' heart. Connection is the humanness of a marriage.

The Disconnected Couple

Tom was a busy physician absorbed in his work. For years Amanda had struggled to bring him back to her, trying to make him stay home, make him talk, and make him be close. The harder she tried, the more resentful she grew. Whatever passion she had once felt began to fade.

When Tom sought counseling his diagnosis of their relationship was pretty accurate. Glancing at Amanda he said, "My marriage has been dead for years, and I've been dead in my marriage. I don't even know if I want to be married anymore." Amanda nodded her head in agreement. She felt like she'd done all the work of the relationship over the years, and she was exhausted from trying to push, pull, and prod her husband to connect.

Tom and Amanda didn't start off that way. Amanda thought Tom was brilliant, charming, and handsome. He made her feel "so important and so loved." Tom said that Amanda had knocked him off his feet when he first met her. She was physically gorgeous, and she also was a woman of intellectual substance. They had shared many of the same values. He just knew that this was the woman God had for him.

> Selfishness is not living as one wants to live. It is always asking others to live as one wishes to live.

Eighteen years later they were in a very different place. In her heart of hearts Amanda "knew" that Tom wouldn't be there for her. Both of them felt alone, empty, and misunderstood. Tom was so tired of being perceived as a marital "failure" by his wife. It was so tempting to turn in the direction of any positive attention elsewhere, especially since every time he turned toward Amanda he felt inadequate. Was there anything he could do to make this woman happy? He doubted it.

Both Amanda and Tom retreated to their own corners to lick their wounds, defensively distancing themselves from the other and blaming the other for the sad state of affairs in their marriage. What could they do? Was there any hope?

From Dave's Journal

Over the years I have come to see that I need to allow Jan to say no or to be angry with me—or both. I want to give her that freedom. At the same time I have had to make it clear that I cannot tolerate disrespect or harshness.

This has been a stretching area for both of us since our goal is to be connected and not to hurt each other.

Transition to Connection

The Apostle Paul longed for connection with the Christians in Corinth:

"We have spoken freely to you, Corinthians, and opened wide our hearts to you. We are not withholding our affection from you, but you are withholding yours from us. As a fair exchange—I speak as to my children—open wide your hearts also" (2 Cor. 6:11–13).

Which of these common ways to avoid connection do you use? Put a check mark by each one that applies to you. Take this chart with you to your support people. Ask God to transform you from a detacher to a connector.

Heart2Heart

1. **From your perspective, what has happened in this marriage that has resulted in the disconnection that both Tom and Amanda are feeling?**

2. **In the past few years in your relationship what things have you done to promote connection that backfired?**

3. **When you think of connection in a marriage, what positive images pop into your mind?**

Him   Her

____ ____ Withdrawal into silence

____ ____ Minimizing how I feel

____ ____ Fudging about how I am really doing

____ ____ Keeping much too active or busy

____ ____ Valuing performance over relationship

____ ____ Projecting my needs onto others and then becoming their caretaker

____ ____ Avoiding connection because of past hurts

____ ____ Seeing my LifeMate as someone hurtful from my past

____ ____ Viewing myself as unlovable

____ ____ Becoming aggressive and argumentative when I get close to my LifeMate or he or she gets close to me

____ ____ Devaluing my LifeMate's feelings, actions, and love

____ ____ Being an independent, "anti-need" hot-shot

____ ____ Spiritualizing pain

Conflicting Human Needs

"A good marriage is one in which the dominant needs are met within the relationship, but where each spouse develops an individual identity, their separate interests, and their own friendships. This may be the most delicate tightrope act in marriage. Extreme independence is as destructive to relationship as total dependence."[2]

Human beings exhibit two conflicting needs when in an intimate relationship. These are the "come close" and "leave me alone" needs. While longing for intimacy, closeness, and a feeling of belonging, we also want to be independent, to control our own destinies, to make our own decisions, and to be free of the demands of others.

Both of these conflicting needs can be met simultaneously in an intimate relationship, but only if we understand boundaries. Good relationships become more wonderful the longer they last, because couples know and honor each other's boundaries.

In every marriage we run into a paradox: We are one and yet not one. It takes two distinct and different LifeMates to create one "us." Oprah asked the Reverend Billy Graham the secret of love. After all, he and Ruth had been married fifty-six years. He smiled and replied, "Ruth and I are happily incompatible!" Our differences make love possible.

Theoretically accepting each of our uniqueness sounds fabulous, but practically it's another issue altogether. Harriet Lerner puts it this way:

> A closed mouth gathers no feet.

> "Humans don't tend to do well with differences. We learn to hate a difference, glorify a difference, exaggerate a difference, deny, minimize or eradicate a difference. We may engage in nonproductive effort to change, fix or shape up the person who isn't doing or seeing things our way."[3]

Boundary lovers are unique. They expect, anticipate, and learn from their LifeMates' differences. They understand that their LifeMates' "otherness" is fundamentally what makes love possible. They dare to explore their differences. They can agree to disagree.

If we understand boundaries, we don't have to keep establishing distance in order to feel safe. No one has to be afraid of being swallowed up by the other. Each LifeMate's need for separateness is understood, and time is created on a joint calendar for this need. At the same time we make certain that our own needs get met. A LifeMate who has clear boundaries is making certain that his or her spouse's are met as well. An unwillingness to accommodate your LifeMate's needs does not necessarily mean that you do not love your spouse, but it does indicate that you value yourself more.

The issue of goodwill toward our LifeMate has been settled. We each are committed to taking ownership for our own lives. Blaming, fixing, changing, and punishing our LifeMates are not in our repertoire. We make it our personal responsibility to grow and live out of our personal value system even if our LifeMates are not operating out of their best selves. If we are angry, we own it as our problem, and we ask, "What do I need to do to work this through?"

Boundary lovers value their LifeMates apart from what they can do. Separateness is viewed as a crucial ingredient in togetherness. Since both LifeMates are free to be themselves, they are free to love and to repair love. Boundaries make for safe connection. Find out how terrific love for two can be! Boundaries require us to face our own tendencies.

Warning: The next personal evaluation may be threatening to your self-perception. Periodically we need to ask ourselves, "What is it like to be in a relationship with me?" Listed below are tendencies that affect the way we relate to our partners. Which of these apply to you? Put a checkmark by any that do.

> **Do I model the kind of behavior I want from my LifeMate or the kind I would expect from an enemy?**

Him   Her

____ ____ Am I easily hurt?

____ ____ Do I like things done "just so"? Is it difficult for me to accept a different way?

____ ____ Is it hard for me to delegate responsibility to someone else?

____ ____ Am I afraid of too much closeness or dependency?

____ ____ Do I fear abandonment?

____ ____ Do I find myself easily jealous?

____ ____ Do I often feel neglected?

____ ____ At times, do I feel that I am being taken advantage of?

____ ____ Am I more critical than I want to be?

____ ____ Do I "walk on eggshells" in order not to upset or anger my LifeMate?

____ ____ Do I constantly put the happiness of others before my own?

____ ____ Do I protect my LifeMate from the consequence of his or her actions?

____ ____ Do I ever begin conversations with "If you really loved me …?

____ ____ Do I get impatient easily? Do I get an edge in my voice when I think my LifeMate should already know something he or she is asking me?

____ ____ Do I have a tough time relaxing until everything on my "To Do" list is accomplished? Am I a bit compulsive?

____ ____ Am I very sensitive to criticism?

____ ____ Do I often feel as if I am being "controlled"?

____ ____ Do I take on too much responsibility?

____ ____ Do I have difficulty saying no?

____ ____ Do I often feel overwhelmed? Do I get tense or "hysterical" when I feel overextended?

____ ____ Do I become anxious about decisions? Do I revisit decisions multiple times after I have made them?

____ ____ Do I ruminate over things for a long time prior to expressing them?

____ ____ Do I give unasked for lectures and advice for my LifeMate's good?

____ ____ Would I describe myself as stubborn?

____ ____ Do I have a tough time admitting when I am wrong?

Take this list to your support people. Chose one tendency. Why do you think that habit got established in your lifestyle? How would your relationship with your LifeMate be affected if you moved against this habitual tendency?

We are to carry our own crosses on a daily basis (Luke 9:23), yet we are to help each other when the burdens of life become overwhelming (Gal. 6:2–5). When we depend on our LifeMates to carry our crosses rather than theirs, we are dependent in an unhealthy way. When we depend on them to do something for us that we need to be doing for ourselves in order to grow into maturity, we become a heavy weight to them. For instance, if I am depending on my LifeMate to make me feel happy or good about myself, I will always be upset at my LifeMate's inadequacy. And my LifeMate will be overwhelmed by my neediness.

Henry Cloud and John Townsend have written some fabulous resources on this topic. *Boundaries in Marriage*[4] is a book that we highly recommend if you desire further reading on this topic. They have defined the things that each of us need to be personally responsible for if we want to be a healthy, fully functioning adult. We are responsible for our own:

Feelings

Attitudes

Behaviors

Choices

Limits: What can I tolerate, what can I not?

Desires: What are the desires of my heart?

Thoughts: I need to guard my thought life.

Values: What are my nonnegotiables?

Talents: What am I doing to develop these?

Love: Whom am I choosing to love? Can I move toward my LifeMate with love even when we are disagreeing or upset, or do I remove my love at those times?

Boundaries define who we are and what our bottom line is. In these ways we exhibit a healthy independence. When we are incapable of this kind of healthy self-sufficiency, fear dominates our marriage. Yet we must balance our independence with a healthy dependence in order to have a healthy interdependence. It must not threaten us to depend on our LifeMate for some of our needs!

Ask for what you need. Anytime we don't ask for what we need, it becomes a secret in our relationship. It is as if there is a wall of resentment between LifeMates, and the one who didn't ask is the only one who is aware of this wall.

A specific request is a preference, not a criticism and not a demand. Remember that because your LifeMate is a separate, unique child of God, he or she has the right to say either "yes" or "no" to your request. In our fantasy world, our LifeMates always say "yes." In the real world, sometimes we are disappointed with their "no."

We depend on our LifeMates to provide us with companionship, to respond to our sexual needs, and to be there with "grace to help in time of need" (Heb. 4:16) when the burdens of life have become overwhelming. We depend on them to broaden our circle of friends, to do their share of family and household maintenance, to parent actively and consistently, and to meet their share of the financial agreements.

Heart2Heart

1. Talk about a time in your marriage when you faced your differences with tolerance, humor, and respect while at the same time maintaining your personal values and voice. What was that like for you?

2. Asking for what we want can make us feel awkward. Talk about which of these excuses you use for not asking for what you want.

If I need to ask I must be weak.
I expect my LifeMate to "just know."
I won't get what I want anyway.
I'm afraid my LifeMate will get mad.
I'm afraid my LifeMate will take my request as criticism.
I'm afraid of not getting what I need if I ask.
What I want is dumb.
I've got it pretty good. I just need to live with it.
I asked before and didn't get what I wanted.
It's not the right time.
I'll just be a bother.
I'm afraid my LifeMate will punish me for days.
I'm not sure how to phrase it.

3. Is there a request that you would like to make to your LifeMate at this time? If so, ask for what you want.

Healthy dependency is a crucial part of a healthy marriage. The challenge in any marriage is to preserve both the "I" and the "we" without losing either, when the going gets tough.

There's a difference between emotional ownership of our own feelings and emotional support for our LifeMates. When we exercise emotional ownership, we have these attitudes:

- I take responsibility for my own feelings, thoughts, and actions.
- I no longer blame my LifeMate for making me feel, think, or act a certain way.
- I acknowledge that no one else can feel my disappointment, guilt, grief, joy, anger, and no one can take it away.
- If my LifeMate is moody, I do not immediately assume it is my fault. I neither blame myself nor attempt to fix the problem. My LifeMate's anger is both his or her choice and problem, just as my anger is my choice and my problem.

Boundaries do not give us a license to be uncaring! When we show emotional support, we have these attitudes:

- I disengage from trying to fix the problem. At the same time I do not become indifferent to my LifeMate.
- I am comforting and supportive. I might listen, hug, or take on a task that would lighten my LifeMate's load.

Freedom is a prerequisite of love. Marriage is about bringing ourselves under the control of God and his principles, not about controlling our LifeMates. It's our LifeMate's life to run deftly, badly, nobly, kindly, cruelly, or lovingly. What we get to choose is our response. Will we let our LifeMates know how we feel? Will we make them aware of what we can or cannot do? Will we adjust our perspective or will we ignore? Setting ultimatums and demanding change doesn't work.

Yet freedom can be scary. It's true that only when we relinquish control are we able to love, to value freedom and choice, and to grow. It's equally true that we can build our relationship by what we do in our separateness, or we can indulge our selfish desires at the expense of our relationship. There are times in every marriage when we question if we really know this person we married.

God himself places such a high premium on our freedom that he doesn't even force us to do things that would be of immense benefit to us. Never will we learn to love or respond to God without that costly freedom.

In marriage, we must follow this example. If we do, we will honor our LifeMate's uniqueness, separateness, and freedom of choice.

If God doesn't force someone to do the right thing, we certainly can't. This means that each of us has to take ownership of our own disappointment, sadness, and helplessness to change our mate. We won't always get what we want.

Each of us needs to learn to grieve rather than getting angry. Why do I need to grieve? Here are just a few reasons. My LifeMate will not change until he or she is ready to. My LifeMate will not always live up to my expectations. In freedom, he or she may limit my options. In freedom, my LifeMate will at times disagree with me, or make a decision, or act in a way that disappoints me.

If I take ownership of my own disappointment, when my LifeMate takes a non-negotiable stand on some issue, I must move from attempting to persuade my spouse to my point of view, to working at accepting his or her choice without making him or her pay. This is the tough stuff of boundaries.

Rate yourself on the following scale in reference to your level of connection. Where do you see yourself on this continuum? Share with your LifeMate.

Heart2Heart

1. What aspects of your LifeMate's uniqueness do you value? Be specific.

2. What separate activities and friends do you enjoy?

3. How does your exercise of freedom and separateness benefit your times of connection?

Red Zone	Yellow Zone	Green Zone
Detached and disconnected. Only conected in anger.	Sometimes close, sometimes distant.	Attached and connected.

Have you noticed that husbands and wives speak different languages? God wired us differently. Different isn't bad, it's just different. At times it's even interesting. One of the major challenges to connection happens when we think like we think, rather than thinking like our LifeMate thinks. Do you fight the differences, or do you seek to understand them, validate them, and even use their style when you are talking with your LifeMate? If you've never tried that, do so. You just might find connection easier.

Read through the following lists of differences between men and women. (This list is a combination of research conducted by H. Norman Wright, John Gray, and Deborah Tannen.) Let your LifeMate know which of these general statements are true of you. Take notes on this conversation. Use your new awareness to more effectively connect with your LifeMate in the future.

1. Women are more inclined to want "feeling" conversations. Men are more inclined toward problem solving. Label the conversation you want to have.
2. Women give and want to hear lots of details. Men go for the bottom line and get straight to the point.
3. Women talk more about people, feelings, and personal issues. Men more often talk about topics such as sports, politics, movies, and so forth.
4. Women want to be liked and included. Men want to be respected and admired.

5. Women who want a LifeMate to understand need to avoid saying, "You don't understand." A man often reacts negatively to that phrase.

6. When a woman says, "Nothing's wrong," something usually is. Offer your services as a sympathetic listener when she is ready to talk.

7. When a woman shares negative emotions, she is generally in the middle of the process of discovering what she feels to be true. She is not stating an objective fact.

8. When a woman has a chance to freely share her feelings, she begins to feel more loving even if she started out tremendously upset.

9. When a woman is upset and emotional, any attempt of her LifeMate's to offer an explanation is taken as invalidation.

10. When a husband initiates a conversation when his LifeMate is upset, it takes away 50 percent of her emotional charge.

11. Men tend to take suggestions as accusations that they've messed up. Barbara De Angelis is credited with the following statements: Men hate to be wrong. They hate being told they are wrong. They hate to suspect that they might have been wrong. And most of all, they hate it when a woman knows that they are wrong before they know it themselves. The tricky part is, men feel they are being "made wrong" or told they did something wrong, when you aren't telling them that at all.

12. A husband feels blamed and defeated when his wife remembers, while a woman feels unloved and neglected when her LifeMate forgets.

13. Men hate unsolicited advice. They presume that their LifeMates believe they don't know what to do or that they can't make it on their own.

14. A husband wants to be part of the solution to a problem; he never wants to be viewed as the problem.

15. LifeMates of either gender may rely more on one of their senses. An intentional connector uses his or her LifeMate's dominant sense when communicating with him or her.

Week 1: Date Night

- Dine in this evening. Perhaps you might enjoy using your love basket.
- Collect a stack of old magazines, three large pieces of bristle board, two glue sticks, and two scissors. Cut out words, phrases, and pictures that represent your personal dreams and your personal goals. Cut out pictures and words that are descriptive of your life now. On one piece of bristle board, create a collage that represents your uniqueness.

Share your collages with each other. Rejoice in each other's uniqueness. Keep the magazines for Dates for Mates, Week # 3 this month.

Week 2: Date Night

Try a restaurant that serves a kind of food that you have never tried before. Enjoy something that stretches you both out of your comfort zone. Often the video store has travel videos. If there is a travel video available of the country that your dining experience may have originated from, watch the video together. Discuss together whether you would ever repeat the experience again or if you might enjoy visiting that country some day.

Week 3: Date Night

It's collage night again. Why don't you order in dinner from your favorite take-out restaurant? Get the piece of bristle board, the old magazines, the glue sticks, and the scissors out. Is there anything you would like to add to your individual collages from two weeks ago? If so, add it. Tonight's goal is to create a collage that represents your "US"— your marital relationship. Cut out words, phrases, and pictures that represent shared dreams, shared goals, and activities that you enjoy together. Rejoice over the shared life you have together. Are there some new dreams, goals, or activities that you would like to share together in the future?

Week 4: Date NIght

Choose a nearby woods, forest, park, or beach and take a hike together. As you walk, describe what you find particularly interesting and beautiful. Take the time to enjoy your surroundings through your partner's eyes. End your walk with a picnic.

FROM PREVIOUS MONTH:

I COMMIT TO PROTECT THE BOUNDARIES
OF OUR MARRIAGE.

**IN MY DESIRE TO LIVE ONE GOOD YEAR
OF MARRIAGE WITH MY LIFEMATE,**

I COMMIT TO CONNECT IN HEALTHY WAYS
ON A DAILY BASIS.

MONTH

SEVEN

"Laughter: Leaving Behind Intensity"

"She wanted a husband and put an advertisement in the personal column. She got two hundred replies, all saying, 'You can have mine!'"

LAUGHTER LOWERS OUR STRESS. Laughter is like oil in a car. Without it, all we get is friction and sparks. If we continue to drive a car without oil, we will burn out the engine.

Laughter can change our moods, raise our spirits, quell fears, and stop tears. Laughter tends to revolutionize our perspectives. Like the sun, laughter can drive winter from the human face. Laughter acts as a buffer against hard times. Humor is to life what shock absorbers are to automobiles. We have to learn to ad-lib our way through turbulence, trials, and touch-and-go situations. If we can laugh together we can get through anything. Life happens!

Laughter helps us learn from experience. There is only one thing

Heart2Heart

1. **Has there been a time when you lost your sense of humor and it did not serve your marriage well?**

2. **What do you appreciate about your LifeMate's sense of humor?**

3. **What is a humorous incident that happened to the two of you that still makes you laugh?**

more painful than learning from experience and that is not learning from experience. Marriages may be made in heaven, but most of the details are worked out and need to be laughed out on earth.

Life has a way of getting us tied up in knots, paralyzed by its seriousness. It's a temptation to take ourselves too seriously.

From Dave's Journal:

To celebrate our twenty-fifth wedding anniversary, we began by spending a week in Napa Valley visiting friends. Since it had been Jan's fantasy to spend the actual night of our twenty-fifth wedding anniversary in a Carmel cottage, we poured over multiple brochures. We finally chose a quaint, thatched roof cottage with an English garden out front.

We arrived around 7:00 p.m. and immediately wondered what we were in for. This was August 7, and the English garden looked like it hadn't been watered since April. An inebriated elderly man pointed us to the registration area. There we found his wife looking as if she was the scientist in "Back to the Future." Her hair looked as if she had stuck her finger in a light socket.

We signed in and proceeded to our cottage, which supposedly had a fireplace. What we saw when we opened the door was a tiny pellet stove balanced precariously on some bricks that looked, frankly, as if it would blow up if we dared light it. As I put the suitcases down, I noticed something moving in the lime green shag carpet. A sense of doom and gloom spread through my body. It isn't every day you have a twenty-fifth wedding anniversary. How in the world was I going to redeem this one? I began by stomping out bugs. I wanted out of this nightmare, so I looked for a phone. You guessed it. There wasn't one.

We had dinner reservations, and we were all too glad to escape. As soon as we placed our order, I got up and went to the phone. I started calling to try to find another option. The bottom line was there was nothing available within a 150-mile radius of Carmel. This was August, prime time in Carmel. We wanted to explore this area so we decided to make the best of it. On the way back from our beautiful dinner, we stopped at the grocery store and bought some bug killer and disinfectant spray.

With trepidation in our hearts, we returned to our "romantic" Carmel cottage, not quite the one we had imagined. It was at that point that Jan informed me that her new negligee was staying in the suitcase. Hooded sweats and socks were her attire for our twenty-fifth wedding anniversary night. We were both laughing when I pulled back the sheets. That's when Jan lost her sense of humor. There on the sheets were silverfish. I said, "Well, that's appropriate, it is our silver wedding anniversary, and there are silverfish."

It took Jan twenty-four hours before she could find any humor in that statement. Life doesn't always turn out the way we anticipate.

Transition to Laughter and Joy

One of the primary tasks of a healthy marriage is to use laughter and humor to keep things in perspective and to renew your love relationship. Laughter is a gift, but it is also a choice, a discipline, and an art. Healthy laughter draws us closer to each other. The couple who learns to laugh feels connected to one another in the midst of life's curve balls and painful realities. The shortest distance between two LifeMates is a smile.

Men and women are wired so differently, but that is no big deal if we haven't lost a sense of humor. Ernie Hoberecht says it well, "After God created the world, He created man and woman. And then to keep the whole thing from collapsing, He created humor."[1]

Has your marriage been enhanced and renewed by laughter? Do you search for joy? Do you initiate both?

> "Never try to guess your wife's size. Just buy anything marked 'petite' and hold onto the receipt."
>
> Barbara Johnson
> ("You said it", Marriage Partnership Summer, 2002 p.11)

Be Open to an Attitude Adjustment

Scripture has much to say about our attitude and its effect on our quality of life.

Heart2Heart

1. **How has your faith affected your face?**

2. **If you believed that laughter and joy are disciplines of the soul, how might your day- to-day existence be different?**

3. **Share a difficult time in your life when faith in God and a sense of humor helped you get through.**

"A cheerful disposition is good for your health; gloom and doom leave you bone-tired" (Prov. 17:22 MSG).

Ecclesiastes says: "There is a right time for everything: A time to cry, a time to laugh, a time to grieve, a time to dance" (Eccl. 3:1, 4 TLB).

"A cheerful heart brings a smile to your face; a sad heart makes it hard to get through the day" (Prov.15:13 MSG).

"It is a wonderful thing to be alive! If a person lives to be very old, let him rejoice in every day of life" (Eccl. 11:7–8 TLB).

"What happiness for those whose guilt has been forgiven! What joys when sins are covered over! What relief for those who have confessed their sins and God has cleared their record" (Ps. 32:1 TLB).

Jesus said, "If your eye is pure, there will be sunshine in your soul" (Matt. 6:22 TLB).

Has the liberation of your spirit fueled a smile on your face, laughter on your lips, and joy in your heart? If it hasn't, maybe you need to notify your face that you have been forgiven. Your slate is clean. You can walk in freedom. It is our prayer that your walk through life will be a collection of laugh lines.

If we learn to laugh at ourselves, we will never run out of material. A misstep can teach us much if we can learn to laugh whenever we stumble, teeter, or fall. We all have to learn to take our commitment to our marriage seriously, but to take ourselves lightly. Ask yourselves a few questions for a glimpse at your own tendencies. What is your first tendency when you make a mistake? When was the last time you were able to laugh at yourself? What happened as a result of your laughter?

Remember that the best thing about being imperfect is the joy it brings to family and friends.

Laughing with others builds confidence, brings people together, and pokes fun at life. Humor often is pain turned into laughter, rather than pain inflicted by laughter. Laughter at others erodes self-esteem, destroys confidence, ruins teamwork, and causes the person being teased to feel dreadfully alone. There is something terribly wrong if, in order to make our candle glow, we find it necessary to snuff out someone else's candle with the use of destructive humor. LifeMates have to be particularly aware of how they talk about their mate to others. It's all too easy to make someone else's foibles the "butt" of our jokes.

Be Alert to Opportunities to Play

When was the last time that you had a fabulously fun time? We hope it wasn't your childhood. We have to give ourselves permission to take a break from planning, soul searching, trying so hard, and from worrying. Play is a vital nutrient in a healthy life. Fun begins with our willingness to look for it, grab it, and transform even the mundane into an opportunity for merriment.

A friend of ours has a T-shirt that says on the front, "Plays Well With Friends!" Do you? Do you have a little child inside of you who has forgotten how to play? In case you have become much too serious, we have listed some great play activities that might be right under your nose.

- Stomp around in some water puddles.
- Play with some Play Doh® or clay.
- Lie on the grass and look at the clouds.
- Revive your Hula-Hoop® skills.

Heart2Heart

1. Talk about a time when someone else used humor to put you down. What effect did this have on you?

2. The next time someone uses humor to put you or someone else down, how are you going to respond? Role-play with each other.

Heart2Heart

1. **What fun activities would you add to your list? Which activities from the above list would not be fun for you?**

2. **What is one of your favorite childhood fun memories?**

3. **Of all your friends, who has the best sense of humor? What effect does this person have on you?**

• Have a watermelon-spitting contest.

• Color in a coloring book.

• Dig around in a garden.

• Roll down a hill.

• Fly a kite.

• Run with abandon.

• Dance in circles at the beach and splash in the waves.

• Visit a tide pool.

• Build a sandcastle.

• Swing on a swing.

• Hang upside down from a jungle gym.

• Go sledding.

• Visit a toy store and buy a toy.

• Lie on the ground at night and count the shooting stars.

• Serve dinner backward. Start with dessert.

• Go ice blocking on a hill at night with friends.

• Meet someone at a plane with a clown nose on.

Be Willing to Try Something New

Jim decided to face his fear and learn to ski. His wife, Debbie, was an avid skier. He said that when he set out that first morning he was facing not only the mountain but an equally daunting mountain of anxiety and fear. Just the process of getting into the gear left him ready for a nap. When he tried to mount the ski lift, Jim fell off and lay prone on the snow, utterly helpless, until a few kind souls took pity on him. By the end of day one, he was feeling a sense of accomplishment because he'd learned how to maneuver the lift and had mastered a gentle slope.

For the next three days Jim persisted until he could be relatively comfortable on the intermediate slope. One of the things he said he had to learn was when to hold on and when to let go. (Sounds like life, doesn't it?)

At first he gripped the bar on the chair lift, held the poles as if they were life jackets, and continually dug his skis into the mountain to slow down and stop. When all else failed, he latched on to his instructor or to unsuspecting fellow skiers. As he gained confidence he began to let the skis run, to permit gravity to perform its magic—"to let go." As the week went on, he pointed the skis downhill more frequently and finally began to get the hang of it.

What kept him going when he wanted to retreat to the lodge for some hot chocolate was that he wanted to be able to ski with his wife. He wanted to get control of his fears. He knew that if he wanted to encourage his child to try new and rewarding activities that could last a lifetime, he had to model it.

We've seen far too many couples who refuse to try anything that brings their LifeMate joy. They'd rather stay in their comfort zone than stretch. That is, until one of them has an affair. Often that becomes the wake-up call in their marriage. When was the last time you dared to try something new? Are you making enough mistakes?

Be Reality-Based

Does your daily life contain enough laughter and joy? Let's take an inventory. Sit down in a quiet spot and list the activities that you do on a normal day. Once your activities are listed, rate each one according to this scale.

Red Zone	Yellow Zone	Green Zone
I hate this. Benefits no one. I do it only because someone would be upset if I stopped. I put no heart into this.	Necessary, but brings me little to no joy. This helps those I love to experience joy. I do these activities as an expression of my love.	This fills me with joy. This is a necessary activity for me and those I love to experience joy. This I do from my heart.

Be a Creative Initiator of Fun!

In order to live longer we need to lighten up. We need to handle all of life's challenges with a chuckle. It certainly beats complaining. Norman

Heart2Heart

"A smile is a curve that sets everything straight!"

Phyllis Diller
(Laffirmations, p. 199)

Cousins coined the term "internal jogging" as a description of laughter. We can be serious without being solemn. Laughter enhances respiration and circulation. It oxygenates the blood, suppresses the stress-related hormones in the brain, and activates the immune system. Even the prospect of a fun event boosts our immune systems.

An assistant professor of family medicine and a researcher in complementary and alternative medicine at the University of California, Irvine, Dr. Lee Berk discovered that even knowing that you will be involved in a positive humorous future event reduces levels of stress hormones in the blood. It also increases levels of chemicals known to aid relaxation. Even the anticipation of play seems to bring balance to our emotional lives.[2]

Fun comes from active, not passive, pursuits, and humor helps us live in the present. Humor is the best way to open doors, minds, and hearts. We are most productive, persistent, creative, and flexible when we are involved in fun activities that bring laughter from deep caverns within us.

Unfortunately, fun can be used in destructive ways. The difference between destructive fun and healthy fun is that destructive fun helps us ignore problems while healthy fun helps us face them. Destructive fun gets boring. We need more and more of it in order to be satisfied. Healthy fun doesn't result in a hangover. If you're having healthy fun, you won't regret it. Healthy fun results in everyone feeling better about his or her self. Destructive fun has the opposite result.[3]

We must not postpone healthy fun. How much priority do you put on creating opportunities for fun, for laughter, and for celebrating life? Memories must be made in the present in order to be enjoyed in the future.

We have a choice. Either we moan and grind our teeth over all the high notes we can't or won't sing, or we leave those to Pavarotti and we sing what we can. If we're into singing we will be active initiators of fun and laughter with a few surprises thrown in.

What fun activities have an energizing effect on the two of you? Have you ever chased each other around the yard or the bedroom, danced to lively music in your own home, squirted each other with hoses, or given each other a massage? We need to liven up the mix from time to time and turn things upside down. When we throw our partners the occasional curve ball, we are not taking them for granted.

It is fun to be surprised. That is how we have been designed. Finding basketball tickets under your pillow or unexpectedly having your favorite music played during dinner, or finding love notes packed in your lunch box. It is the random, unanticipated surprises that bring joy to our hearts.

A LifeMate was married to a guy who loved to take things apart and then put them back together again. She decided to get him a fancy VCR for his birthday. She took it apart and gave it to him wrapped in sixteen different boxes.[4]

Friends of ours had their picture taken with Nancy Reagan. They gave us the photo. We had our friends sign it. We framed it and hung it on our wall. The people who caught the joke, laughed.

We have a dear friend who had to have half of her colon removed. Her husband now calls her his "little semicolon."

Do something to inject playfulness and laughter into your sex life today. Sex is supposed to be fun. Laughter shared by lovers is a powerful aphrodisiac. It defuses nervousness and inhibition. It keeps the juices

Heart2Heart

1. What have you learned about your daily activities from taking this inventory?

2. Are there activities that aren't fun for you and yet need to be done to keep life for yourself and those you love running smoothly? What could you do to inject a little fun into the mundane?

3. Are there activities that you need to drop? How will you face the person who will be disappointed?

flowing. Love and laughter need to be natural bed partners. Make a love "play date" with your LifeMate. Show up with chocolate flavored body paint, a feather boa, and some lotion. After you pick him up off the floor, who knows what might happen?

Heart 2 Heart

1. Create a list of people who make you both laugh.

2. Create a list of movies that make you both laugh.

3. How do you feel about surprises? How might you enjoy being surprised and surprising your LifeMate?

4. Take some "jest medicine." Once a week over dinner, share a joke that you learned that week. Write the great ones in a "jest journal."

Rate yourself on the following scale in reference to your level of humor connection. Where do you see yourself on this continuum? Share with your LifeMate.

Red Zone	Yellow Zone	Green Zone
I have no sense of humor	I am developing a sense of humor.	I laugh easily and often.

Our neighbor was having a garage sale while her husband Norm was away on a business trip. In the process of going through her house, she came across her husband's red silk shirt from the 60s. Every once in a while he would wear it to a neighborhood party. She absolutely hated the shirt. With great delight she gave it a prime spot in the garage sale. The next door neighbor saw it on display and bought it. He knew how much Norm loved this shirt. Life went on as normal until we were all invited to Norm's birthday party. Norm began opening his gifts. The guy next door presented him with a gorgeously wrapped package. You guessed it; in the package was Norm's beloved red silk shirt. Everybody roared, even Norm's wife, although she did threaten the neighbor with bodily harm.

Week 1: Date Night

Have a great dinner together and then go to your favorite card store. Check out all the humorous cards that you might give your LifeMate.

Read the cards together and laugh. Then put them back where you got them. It's a "cheap date."

Week 2: Date Night

Have a night at home watching home videos and looking through photo albums of your childhood. We have a hunch you'll find some comedy there. Accompany it with your favorite dessert.

Week 3: Date Night

Go to a comedy club if there is one in your area. If not, rent a stand-up comedian's video. Make some popcorn if this date happens at home. Laugh until you cry!

Week 4: Date Night

Go to your favorite bookstore and find the humor section. Take turns reading your favorite jokes or stories to each other. Make sure you get a cup of cappuccino or something equally decadent to make it special.

FROM PREVIOUS MONTH:

I COMMIT TO CONNECT IN HEALTHY WAYS

ON A DAILY BASIS.

> **IN MY DESIRE TO LIVE ONE GOOD YEAR**
> **OF MARRIAGE WITH MY LIFEMATE,**
>
> I COMMIT TO MAKING JOY AND LAUGHTER
> PART OF OUR RELATIONSHIP.

MONTH
EIGHT

"Teamwork: Leaving Behind the Power Struggle"

"Individuals play games, but teams win championships!"

Sign in the locker room of the New England Patriots

JUST ABOUT EVERYTHING WE ACCOMPLISH in life depends on teamwork. Why, even sex is a team sport!

Teamwork involves pulling together, planning together, praying together, proceeding together. Teamwork involves developing shared values, shared vision, and mutually beneficial goals. Teamwork embraces each other's perspectives and maximizes each other's strengths. At times teamwork requires functioning independently for the good of the team. Teamwork shares the credit for victories and the blame for losses. Teamwork provides more resources, ideas, and energy than one person working alone. Teamwork requires a shift from "working against" to "working with."

Marriage can be the ultimate cooperative adventure. Couples who choose to be LifeMates for a lifetime have taken the words "for better or worse" to heart. There is no escape hatch. Knowing that both partners cooperate for the mutual benefit of each other and the marriage, they don't get derailed by the bumps. Their stubborn determination to create a thriving partnership creates a positive momentum of its own. Cooperation doesn't mean that one person accommodates every wish and demand of the other in order to keep the peace. Teamwork must be willingly embraced by both LifeMates. It is fully committed to creating an "us" that works for both of them. If there is a team plan, two LifeMates are working the plan. That's the beauty of teamwork.

> Ultimately the marriage loses when one person feels defeated.

Teamwork Lived Out

Carrie Brown runs an old fashioned general store on Highway 128 in the wine country of Sonoma, California called the Jimtown Store. On July 4, 1987, while visiting friends and relatives, Carrie and her husband, Werner, came across an abandoned, 100-year-old cluster of buildings with a "For Sale" sign out front. When they walked in, their imagination was captured. They felt like they had stepped back in time.

Within a month, the two New York artists had made the decision to move to Sonoma to start a new life. It took a year and a half to buy the place and another year to remodel it. Together, Carrie and Werner, working as a team, remodeled and refurbished the store that finally opened on Memorial Day, 1991.

Seven years later Werner was diagnosed with lung cancer. The prognosis was not good. He died December 2000. Carrie describes her husband this way, "He was the most generous, inclusive person. He looked on me as an equal. We always did things as a team, and he gave me the confidence to carry on without him."[1] In the two years before he died Werner worked with Carrie on the store and on the Jimtown Store cookbook. For her forty-fifth birthday, Werner took Carrie to Greece. She couldn't in her wildest dreams have imagined what he had in store for her there.

On the first evening in Greece they went out for dinner. Suddenly, to her surprise, twenty-one people from all different stages in her life showed up. They each wore a ribbon. They were Carrie's presents! Werner knew Carrie would need a strong support system to face the harsh realities that lie ahead. When he died a year later, these people embraced her, encouraged her, and challenged her to keep going. An unusual couple. A magnificent team!

Different Types of Teams

This is far from the norm. It is extremely rare for a couple to start out as a partnership team. They may start out as a hierarchical team where the strongest in personality or voice thinks that his or her way of doing things makes the most sense. Dominant partners have difficulty hearing their LifeMates' perspectives and may even spiritualize their own positions.

The truth is the other LifeMate's way is different. Differences aren't wrong. They're just different. Nevertheless, in the hierarchical team one of you sets the agenda, and the other scurries around to make the agenda happen. The team is not about "us"; the team is about one person, either the "he" or the "she." That person makes all the decisions and calls all the shots. That person take a one-up position in the marriage.

The LifeMate who feels one-down in this hierarchical team begins to see that no matter how he or she chooses words, no matter the speaking tone, the dominant LifeMate does not welcome input. It is minimized, discounted, ignored, or presented as the other's idea.

It is not unusual, at that point in time, for the low partner on the totem pole to start to aggressively push a separate agenda. In fact this partner can begin to devalue the other's perspective just as his or her perspective was devalued. In an attempt not to be controlled, the low partner becomes controlling. At that point the team gets competitive, and a power struggle ensues. Will it be "my way" or "your way"? Both partners are invested in the bottom line being "my way."

Another option is called a partnership team. This is where we both work to discover another possibility: "our way." Both are invested in the marriage being a double win.

This is the stage where partners work with each other, not for each other. They check in rather than checking up on each other. The truth is, if you are married you are a team. The question is, what kind of a team?

Heart**2**Heart

1. What kind of a team have you created in the recent years of your marriage?

   Hierarchical

   Competitive

   Partnership

2. Is your team big enough for two? How open are you to your LifeMate's perspective?

3. What one thing could you do that would move you in the direction of a partnership?

From Jan's Journal:

There was a time in our marriage when wedlock turned into deadlock. We were caught in a tug of war, a power struggle. Neither of us was willing to be influenced by the other, and we were deathly afraid of being controlled by the other.

One of the primary areas that this showed was in my inability to listen to Dave. Either I was like a Teflon ® pan deflecting everything he said and refusing to let it stick, or I was in a suit of armor completely defended and at alert, blocking his attempts at communication. The feeble attempts I made at listening amounted to "grasshopper listening." I would listen just long enough to hear what I expected and then jump in with my perspective. In my attempts not to be controlled, I became reactive and controlling.

From Dave's Journal:

There was a reason Jan was so reactive. Early on in our marriage, I had adopted an attitude based on input about leadership that I received from our pastor. I was not overbearing or cruel. I didn't come on like gangbusters. I would consider what I thought Jan's needs were, but bottom line, I just wanted her to back off, let me handle things, and make the decisions. I didn't want her to muddy up the waters with a differing perspective. I wanted her to trust me and let me take charge. (If she had done that, we would have lived happily ever after! Right! We certainly wouldn't be writing this book.)

As you no doubt have realized, we both had become intolerant of differences. We perceived them as a threat. Our marriage was not big enough for two perspectives. We were not working as a team.

What Is a Power Struggle?

Even though you love one another, do you sometimes find it hard to live with each other because you're so different? Welcome to marriage! Can you relate to any of these examples?

- "I'm a morning person, and she's a night person. On the weekend it is absolutely frustrating that half the day is shot before we can do anything."
- "I want to save as much money as possible for retirement. She feels it's important to get long-term health insurance in case one of us is disabled. I am absolutely adamant and refuse to spend the money. She is tempted to charge it, but hasn't yet."
- "He wants to downsize. I want to buy a bigger house so all the grandchildren can come and stay comfortably."
- "I bring my kids into the new blended family. She brings 'her' kids. We scan the horizon looking for inequity of treatment. Then we take out our feelings on each other and on the kids."

"We had a conversation about house-work and agreed on who does what. Now we are a NAG FREE ZONE."

Power struggles happen anytime that one of you asks for something or brings up something that the other one isn't willing to consider. Instantly it becomes a "my way" versus "your way" dilemma. A power struggle ensues.

A power struggle leads to a self-righteous arrogance about "my way" of doing things. It inhibits two things that are crucial in a healthy marriage: an honest self-examination and a willingness to say, "I'm sorry."

Then you believe that your LifeMate is against you and isn't hearing what you are trying to say. You start to act like inept attorneys. You argue your point so long and hard that you wear your LifeMate down. Unfortunately in marriage it is not healthy to have a "winner" and a "loser." Ultimately the marriage loses when one person feels defeated.

Heart2Heart

1. What issues in your relationship often leave the two of you deadlocked in a power struggle?

2. Was there a time when you operated as a partnership? Describe.

3. How did that feel?

A power struggle is a pivotal turning point in a marriage. How we handle the power struggle determines whether we will be team players or adversaries. If we both care and are honest about our viewpoints, then it is inevitable that we will be tempted to engage in a power struggle. Seldom do two "I's" see an issue the same way.

When the two of you aren't communicating well and that is unusual, HALT! Ask if either of you are hungry. Angry? Lonely? Tired? If so, take care of those needs first, and then go back to the discussion.

Teamwork Blockers

Review the ten "Teamwork Blockers" listed below together. Put a check mark beside any of the ten blockers that one or both of you have brought to your marriage relationship recently.

1. Misunderstanding of what is yours to control; the belief that you have the power, and it is your right to change the actions or the attitudes of your LifeMate.

2. Believing that the area of decision making is your only opportunity to assert your individuality in your marriage.

3. Misunderstanding of the difference between influence and control. When you perceive every statement by your LifeMate as an order (control), you will block all input (influence) and your team shuts down.

4. Believing that if you are open to and go along with your LifeMate's suggestion, you are being controlled.

5. Refusing to move out of your comfort zone. If marriage requires you to grow in an area that you have never previously considered and you refuse, your team suffers.

6. Conflicting values and vision. These take you in opposite directions, and there can be no teamwork.

7. Rigidity, inflexibility, and selfishness. If you believe that your way is the only way and that you must always be right, then you are not a team player. If marriage is all about "you" there can be no "us."

8. Lack of responsibility. When one LifeMate fails to follow through on a promise or commitment, the team suffers.

9. Habit of triangulating. When there is a difference between you, you bring in another person to support your perspective, and your team gets nowhere.

10. Misunderstanding of conflict. If you believe all disagreement and conflict is destructive, then you effectively short-circuit discussion and your team suffers.

11. Inability to admit your own needs and limitations. If you don't ever admit you need help, your LifeMate will assume you don't.

12. Secretiveness. If you want to maintain the upper hand by withholding information, or lying, there is no possibility of teamwork. If you

REMEMBER: The goal is more important than the role. Would you be willing to take a subordinate role in order to accomplish a team goal?

Heart2Heart

1. Share one team blocker that you believe you need to drop.

2. Give an example of a time when that blocker got in the way of a discussion the two of you were having.

3. Think back to your last argument. Which team blockers might have been in operation? Attempt to revisit that discussion with a willingness to hear your LifeMate's perspective.

are embarrassed to admit you made a mistake, or that you are inadequate to perform the task, teamwork ceases.

If we come into a conflict with any of these teamwork blockers operating, we will find ourselves locked in a power struggle.

Characteristics of Team Players!

John C. Maxwell in his book, *The 17 Essential Qualities of a Team Player: Becoming the Kind of Player Every Team Wants*,[2] lists the characteristics of effective teammates. Put a checkmark by the ones that are true of you.

Him   Her

____ ____ ADAPTABLE: "Blessed are the flexible for they shall not be bent out of shape."

____ ____ COLLABORATIVE: Ability to work together enthusiastically to accomplish the team's goals; not just out for self. Seeks mutual benefit and mutual satisfaction.

____ ____ COMMITTED: Person is 100 percent on board and loyal. The escape hatch is locked.

____ ____ COMMUNICATIVE: Willing to listen and learn, able to talk with respect.

____ ____ COMPETENT: In areas of strength, has knowledge and skill.

____ ____ DEPENDABLE: Can be counted on. Trust what they commit to do will be completed.

____ ____ DISCIPLINED: Accomplishes what they really don't want to do so that they can focus on what they really want to do.

____ ____ ENLARGING: Values and encourages each other's goals and dreams.

____ ____ ENTHUSIASTIC: A positive force striving for excellence.

____ ____ INTENTIONAL: Works with purpose. Says no to things that cause them to stray from their purpose.

____ ____ MISSION-CONSCIOUS: Places team accomplishment ahead of individual accomplishment.

____ ____ PREPARED: Diligent in preparation. No mistake is wasted.

____ ____ RELATIONAL: Values the give and take of being a team player. Values their teammates and lets them know it. Treats others with understanding and respect.

____ ____ SELF-IMPROVING: Is teachable, and is dedicated to developing personal strengths.

____ ____ SELFLESS: Doesn't care who gets the credit.

____ ____ SOLUTION-ORIENTED: Dedicated to the belief that together we can find a solution.

____ ____ TENACIOUS: Persevering. Believes hard times are no time to quit trying.

Rate yourself on the following scale in reference to your level of connection. Where do you see yourself on this continuum? Share with your LifeMate.

Heart2Heart

1. Get together with your LifeMate. Point out the characteristics of being an effective team player that you see in your spouse.

2. Share with your LifeMate the one characteristic of a team player that you would like to develop personally. Then commit to intentionally focus on that characteristic in the next month with your support person.

3. At the end of every week ask your LifeMate, "How have I done as a team player this week?" Affirm progress.

Red Zone	Yellow Zone	Green Zone
Danger: Is there a team?	Teamwork in some areas.	Effective team player.

Transition to Teamwork!

Starting over requires that we become "teamwork builders" rather than "teamwork blockers." Habits are hard to break. Contact your accountability people, ask them to pray for you and support you as you attempt to become team players and break free of your negative blocking patterns.

Teamwork Builders

1. A belief that even though change is difficult, it is worth it, and that character is more important than comfort. By contrast, if our only desire is to stay comfortable and never change, then each LifeMate's limitations and immaturities inhibit our relationship. If this is happening, then the least mature and the most insecure part of each of us rules our marriage. That creates its own problems.

2. I let go of the demand that this issue be solved "my way." Am I open to the thought that there is always more to learn and there might be a different way that would be more effective?

3. I seek to understand my LifeMate's position even if my anxiety is going through the roof. I listen to learn. I listen for the reasons behind that perspective. I get as much detail as possible. I do not truly understand until I can verbalize the position to my LifeMate's satisfaction.

4. I breathe deeply. I talk in a softer tone. If I am having difficulty regulating my emotions, I can control my behavior. Teeth marks on my tongue are a tremendous sign of maturity. If I can't regulate my emotions, I will take a time-out.

5. I refuse to attack, rage, or withdraw as a way of calming my anxiety and as an attempt to control my LifeMate. I refuse to dominate. If I find myself angry, I confront the issue promptly and constructively. I do not, under any circumstances, attack or withdraw from my LifeMate.

6. I demonstrate respect for my LifeMate's right to express a difference.

7. I remind myself that my LifeMate is attempting to influence me toward change, not control me. I have a choice!

8. I list my LifeMate's concerns on a piece of paper.

9. I take a courageous step toward intimacy. I speak my truth in a positive, nonadversarial way about what my perspective is and the reasons behind it. I maintain my position calmly. I remember to use positive, specific, active requests that in no way point to any failure on my LifeMate's part.

10. I list my own concerns on a piece of paper.

11. I ask myself, "Do I really care?" If I don't care very much about this issue and my LifeMate does, I embrace my LifeMate's position.

12. If I care deeply about the issue, I create a master list of the concerns that are important to both of us. Remember, the goal is a collaborative alliance where I win, my LifeMate wins, and the marriage relationship wins. The object is to find a third alternative that will satisfy both of us.

Heart**2**Heart

1. In what ways in your marriage have you been a team builder?

2. Are there any beliefs that you need to adopt in order to become a more efficient teamwork builder? Be specific.

3. Are there new actions that you need to implement in order to be an effective team builder?

A Tough Teamwork Challenge!

If your LifeMate raises an issue about you personally, STOP! Breathe deeply! Confront yourself. Ask yourself, "Is this an area in which I need to grow? Is this a blind spot? Have I in anyway been reticent to move out of my comfort zone? By remaining there have I let myself or my LifeMate down? Is it possible that for the good of all—me, my LifeMate, and our marriage, I need to submit enthusiastically on this one?"

Thank your LifeMate for the feedback. Repeat the feedback. Grapple with the input. Is this a needed area of growth? If it is, take it to your support person, and let your LifeMate know you are working on this.

If you don't think it is a needed area of growth, run it by your support person anyway and get the input. Go back to your LifeMate with your perspective. When faced with the anxiety of staying the same or the anxiety of growth, always choose the direction of growth.

How Does Our Team Handle Mistakes and Failures?

If you came home from work and discovered that your LifeMate had absentmindedly driven through your garage door, how would you react?

a. Attack your LifeMate for stupidity.

b. Get sarcastic and insinuate your LifeMate needs to go back to driving school with your adolescents.

c. Rail on your LifeMate about the amount of money it was going to cost to get a new paint job on the car and repair the garage door.

d. Phone all your friends and make fun of your LifeMate.

e. Hug your LifeMate, ask if your LifeMate is okay and say that he or she is worth more to you than the car and the garage door.

f. A through D

g. All the above.

How we handle each other's mistakes is a make-it-or-break-it issue for couples. If we attack each other for making a mistake, our team is annihilated. Effective teams learn from mistakes. Realistic teams expect mistakes. After all, we are human and humans make mistakes. Marriage stretches both of us way outside of our comfort zones and that's when it's easy to trip up. When one of us makes a mistake, members of a partnership team stand alongside the other and ask, "What can we both learn from this?"

Read the following teamwork inventory together. Put a checkmark by the areas where teamwork shows up in your marriage right now. (Teamwork does not mean that you necessarily share equally in each area. Because of your individual giftedness and experience, the team may decide that one of you is a natural to handle that area. Nevertheless, that area is discussed as a team and both of you could handle the area if life required that of you.)

____ Choosing how we spend our leisure time

____ Deciding how to celebrate special occasions

____ Deciding where to go on vacation

____ Deciding where and when to relocate

____ Deciding how we relate to our adult children

____ Deciding how involved we are with extended family

____ Deciding the issues related to caregiving with parents

____ Deciding how often we entertain

____ Deciding where we worship

____ Deciding the amount of involvement in church-related activities

____ Deciding about ministry involvement

____ Deciding how much time we spend with separate friends

____ Doing indoor household chores

____ Doing outdoor chores

____ Doing maintenance tasks

____ Doing grocery shopping

____ Deciding how much money to save

____ Making major purchases inside our home

____ Making major purchases outside our home

____ Deciding how much and where to invest

____ Deciding how our bills are handled

____ Deciding how much to contribute to charity or church

____ Deciding how to disperse our inheritance

____ Deciding about health care issues

____ Sharing intimate sexual times

____ Deciding where we each work

____ Deciding the hours we each work

In what areas are the two of you functioning as a team in your marriage? If there are few to no areas in which teamwork is operating, what one area might you like to approach as a team? If there is an area in which you would like to see greater teamwork, what would that be? How would your marriage benefit by greater teamwork in this area?

Week 1: Pillow Talk

1. If the two of you were going to come up with a name for your team, what might it be? Brainstorm together.

2. Why does your team exist? What difference is it going to make to the two of you and your world that you are married? Together create a mission statement for your team. In our book, *LifeMates: A Lover's Guide for a Lifetime Relationship*, (Cook Communications, 2001) we asked a few couples to share their mission statements. Here are a few samples:

    "To magnify God together."

    "To wisely develop and use our time, talents, and resources to help others."

    "To build healthy, loving relationships in which we help each other become our best selves."

    "To have fun."

    "To be partners who love, cherish, honor, and enjoy each other."

3. In the course of a "normal week" who are all the people that our team interacts with in one way or another? Make a list. These people are being influenced by your marital team.

Week 2: Pillow Talk

1. What are five strengths that your LifeMate brings to your team that you value? Acknowledge the top three contributions by your LifeMate to your family's well-being. Express your gratitude for these contributions.

2. What are the goals the two of you are working toward at this time? If you are not moving toward a goal, together decide on one. Write it down. Pray over it.

3. How can you each use your strengths to move the team closer to your goal or goals?

Week 3: Pillow Talk

1. What are the five most important things that, from your perspective, make a house a home? This may be anything from getting to watch

TV together in bed; to having snacks while watching a movie or a sporting event on TV; to entertaining friends on a regular basis; to having bathrooms that are sparkling clean. There is no wrong answer. Voice your preferences.

2. List each other's top five things. Ask each other, "How many of these are we already implementing in the way we do life?"

3. How could our team cooperate to help one of the new items from each of our lists become a reality in our home by the end of the month?

Week 4: Pillow Talk

1. What is one thing that is causing you each concern right now? It could be personal, marital, or parental. Write both of your concerns down.

2. Brainstorm at least three different scenarios for how this could be effectively handled. Do this for each of your concerns.

3. Rate the scenarios. Decide on a plan of action for one month. Commit to revisit these issues in a month to see if your team is with pleased with the resolution. Set a date, and put it on both of your calendars to talk about.

FROM PREVIOUS MONTH:
I COMMIT TO MAKING JOY AND LAUGHTER
PART OF OUR RELATIONSHIP.

**IN MY DESIRE TO LIVE ONE GOOD YEAR
OF MARRIAGE WITH MY LIFEMATE,**

I COMMIT ON A DAILY BASIS TO BE A TEAM
PLAYER IN OUR RELATIONSHIP.

MONTH
NINE

"Faith: Leaving Behind Religion"

> "The strength of a man consists in finding out the way in which God is going and going in that way too"
>
> **Henry Ward Beecher[1]**

WHEN BOTH LIFEMATES ARE DEDICATED to becoming the man or woman God wants them to be, God becomes the One who is ultimately in charge. Each LifeMate will change because God desires it, not because his or her LifeMate deserves it. Our personal limitations then will not be the limitations of the marriage. As each LifeMate follows through with the day-to-day work that Christ asks of him, he grows, and as a result his marriage grows. This doesn't happen instantly. We are all in process. As we let God have more of us, he is ready to give us more of himself. Our LifeMates can't help but benefit.

A growing mutual faith solidifies our marriage. Authenticity increases. We each experience a deeper more intimate understanding of what is on each other's heart. We have fewer masks that we hide behind, and because of that we are more relaxed and more connected. Love for each other increases. It feels tangible. As trust increases so do feelings of safety and security. It is transforming to pray for our LifeMates and to know that they are holding us up to the Lord in prayer.

As we grow in our spiritual intimacy we become more grateful people. Together we verbalize on a regular basis all the blessings God has given to us. We begin to see God's active intervention in our relationship.

Together we become more aware of the needs of others. As we pray together for others and minister together to touch others, our sense of purpose increases. Our dream becomes higher than the American dream. Together, we can better handle life and all it throws at us. The condition of our heart becomes evident through our attitudes and actions. Together, as a couple, we can make a difference for eternity. As a result of developing spiritual intimacy, LifeMates are knit together.

> Religion is for those who are afraid to go to Hell,
> Spirituality is for those who have been there.

The Drifting Couple

When Renee and Martin got married, Renee anticipated times of intense spiritual connection. After all, before marriage, Martin was active in his church and in Inter-Varsity Christian Fellowship. After marriage all she got was disappointment. Martin seemed passive and unmotivated. She felt cheated, got angry, and then she would hit him with a tactless guilt trip such as, "If you were the spiritual leader you're supposed to be, our marriage would be better." Martin resented her barbs and distanced from Renee and from God.

They both believed in the Bible, but they were tired, distracted, and angry at the other's inertia and lack of spiritual motivation. They went to church fairly regularly, but it seemed to them that so many Christians weren't walking their talk. The pastor would give them a welcoming hug, but his eyes were always casing the crowd to see if anyone better was coming along. Their church had been through an ugly split over doctrinal issues. And the leader of the "Young Marrieds" class had to step down because he'd had an emotional infatuation with one of the young women in the class.

Early in their marriage Renee and Martin had tried unsuccessfully to have children. Their hearts still ached about that. Their prayers had become routine, but they secretly wondered if their words went any higher than the ceiling. What were they to do?

Heart2Heart

1. From your perspective, what might have led to the spiritual slump that this couple is facing?

2. Over the years of your marriage, what has led you to times of spiritual disconnection?

3. What has been different about the times that your spiritual relationship was a cementing force in your marriage?

From Jan's Journal:

Moments, millions of moments make up a marriage. Of all our marriage moments, the ones I most treasure are moments when I sink into David's arms in bed and he begins to pray for me, for our family, and for those whose concerns we lift up to our Savior. At times we lie in silence together in God's presence. At times we both voice prayers of gratitude, and at other times we conversationally talk together to God. These moments do more to make me feel centered, secure, intimate, and treasured than any other moments of my day. Truly, our prayer times knit us together in love.

From Dave's Journal:

After a great deal of struggle in this area, and more than our share of failures in consistent Bible reading, we have found something that works for us. Separately we read the same passage of Scripture on a daily basis. We both approach the passage with two questions: What does it show me about God? What do you want from me, Lord? Before we go to sleep at night, I share my insights and then encourage Jan to share hers. We each also share if there are things we don't understand and if there are matters we need to confess. Then we pray together. This works for us because separately we both are hungry for all of God, and yet we need to be held accountable to stick to the discipline of a "quiet time." Some couples seem to be able to have their devotional time together on a daily basis. That didn't work well for us. Our study habits are different, and our schedules are often in conflict.

Growing spiritually as LifeMates does not mean:
- We will never argue, struggle, disagree, disappoint, or lose it with each other.
- We will be immune from trouble, from an affair, from divorce.
- We will feel connected and in love all the time.
- We will always see eye to eye.
- Our marriage will be one intense happiness feast.
- We will no longer be irked by each other's differences.
- We will discover a mystical and emotional reality most of the time.
- We will never hurt each other again.
- We will only need the Bible and each other.
- We will fit someone else's definition of a Christian couple.
- We will always feel close and intimate with God and each other.

William James wrote of "once born" and "twice born" people. "Once born" sail through life without anything that shatters or complicates their faith. For them, God is a benevolent, benign influence who keeps their world neat and orderly. But "twice born" souls are people who are tested, doubt God's providence through some event, and then regain their faith. They are forever changed; they are stronger. For the twice born, God is the power who enables them to keep going in a stormy and dangerous world. Alcoholics Anonymous offers this profound saying: "Religion is for those who are afraid to go to Hell, spirituality is for those who have been there."

Life is a journey. We can be fearful tourists sticking to well-worn paths, hoping that the ride will be safe rather than daring to sail in uncharted waters. Yet the healthiest LifeMates are those out on the edge of the rock—prodding one another, challenging each other, propping one another up, and marveling at the unknowable—a great and mighty God. Sometimes we must be willing to get rid of the life we expected, so as to experience the life that is waiting for us!

Heart2Heart

Create a graph of your spiritual journey from birth until the present.

1. What meaningful times stand out to you? What has brought on the questioning times and times of doubt? What can you say about the times of disbelief?

2. When has your faith been tested?

3. What would you say were the character building times in your life?

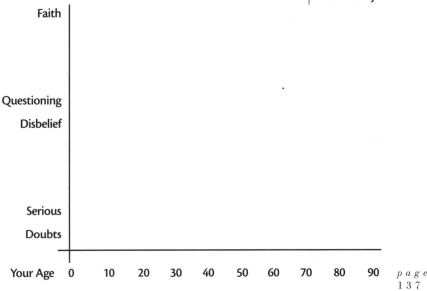

Under the different ages, write words to remind you of significant events that influenced your spiritual development or lack of it in each of the three categories.

Heart2Heart

1. What has suffering taught you about living?

2. Have you had to make your way back to faith at some point in time? When? What was that process like for you? How did you regain your faith?

3. What are some good things that have come out of that process?

We can't give what we haven't received. Without Christ's influence in our lives, we don't know how to love—really love. We only know how to act out of duty, how to fake it, and how to take it.

Lee and Leslie Strobel in their excellent book, *Surviving a Spiritual Mismatch* share the following seven reasons why God must be first:

• We keep God first because he deserves our primary allegiance.

• We keep God first because this perspective recalibrates our life.

• We keep God first because he will meet needs that our spouse never could.

• We keep God first because he empowers us to love our spouse when he or she's not lovable.

• We keep God first because he can create something good from the pain of our mismatch.

• We keep God first because he will be our spouse when our earthly spouse is distant.

• We keep God first because he loves our partner even more than we do.[2]

Only as we love Jesus more than we love each other do we have the love for each other. We then become channels of God's love. There is something far more important in our marital relationships than pleasing each other or making each other happy. We are to put Christ first in both of our individual lives, so together we will love the Lord and become his channel to those in our lives.

Years ago Charlie and Martha Shedd asked these questions in a marvelous book, *Celebration in the Bedroom*. We have kept these in our daily planners since we first read them. They challenge us. What about you?

- "The fruit of the Spirit is love." Is there an increasing concern for each other in our marriage?
- "The fruit of the Spirit is joy." Are there increasing seasons of gladness in our relationship?
- "The fruit of the Spirit is peace." Is there an increasing quiet in our hearts, in our home, and in our lives?
- "The fruit of the Spirit is longsuffering." Is there an increasing stretch in our attitudes?
- "The fruit of the Spirit is gentleness." Are we increasingly kind, more courteous, and softer in our touch?
- "The fruit of the Spirit is meekness." Is there a growing self-honesty in each of us?
- "The fruit of the Spirit is goodness." More and more, do we seek to be a blessing?
- "The fruit of the Spirit is faith." These fears of ours, are they on the decline?
- "The fruit of the Spirit is temperance." Are we more and more in charge of our emotions?[3]

Heart**2**Heart

Answer these questions separately and then discuss them together.

Why am I here?

Where am I going?

Does life have meaning for me? If so, what meaning?

What do I believe about God?

What do I believe about Jesus?

What values would I die for?

What do I believe about the Bible?

How do I see other Christians?

What do I do with the cross?

What do I believe about the church and church attendance?

LifeMates grow toward faith in their own way and in their own time. Trying to push, fix, or control a LifeMate's spiritual journey will only cause our LifeMate to isolate.

Praying for God to change our LifeMate is futile. Why? Not because God isn't capable. We need to pray that God will change us, that he will reveal our weaknesses, our sins, our rotten thinking, our unrealistic expectations and that he will dig out the root of bitterness in us.

Ask yourselves this question: How are we doing in expressing (through words and actions) our faith as a living reality in front of our friends?

If You Are Both Believers and Unequally Yoked

Ideally, marriage is a covenant to mutual growth. However, what do you do if you have a hunger and thirst for God but your mate does not have that same desire? What if you feel as if you're married to a spiritual giant, and you are a new Christian? Hebrews 5:12–14 and 1 John 2:12–14 talk of levels of spiritual progress involving the infant, the youth, and the parent.

Sharon Drury wrote a thought-provoking article to women struggling with spiritual imbalances in their marriages in Partnership magazine years ago. We paraphrase her wisdom with the prayer that your marriage will be strengthened by it.

If you are spiritually more advanced than your mate, have patience. We all go through seasons. We're in process. None of us are finished products, thank the Lord. Don't judge your mate by your standards. Remember, acceptance is the only thing that leaves our spouses free to grow. Critique your own life rather than your mate's. Honestly affirm and esteem your mate for his or her good points. Perhaps you are not personally challenged enough. Maybe there is a place for your talent in the game rather than using all your energy to boo from the grandstand. Confess your prideful attitude to God and ask the forgiveness of your mate.

Perhaps you feel like a spiritual ant in comparison to your spouse. We want you to know that you can change some ineffective habits. This is not a competition; it is a communion with your God. Is Christ central in your life? If he is, your husband won't be. Take your hubby off the pedestal, and put God on. Remember the theme—progress, not perfection. God is your help, so avoid knocking yourself down based on some unspoken "should." Get involved in mentoring someone who is a new Christian. He or she will keep you on your toes and accountable to steadily grow at your own pace.[4]

If You Are Unequally Yoked

When one of you accepts Christ as your personal Savior, your relationship changes. Disequilibrium strikes a relationship. This can be frightening for both of you. Change almost guarantees that the person closest to you will try his or her hardest to push you back into your old ways of life. Every relationship seems to have an equilibrium, and when one mate initiates any change, the other often struggles to maintain the status quo.

If you are married to a non-Christian, and perhaps reading this book alone, you have a tremendous influence. Allow the Holy Spirit to make you into the most loving LifeMate. Your silent contribution to your marriage will be the best way of convincing your spouse to become a believer (1 Pet. 3:1–2).

There are no guarantees that your LifeMate will accept the Lord, however. For your own sake, as well as for the sake of your marriage, maintain your commitment to be in communion with God, to obey him, and then to minister to your spouse at every opportunity. Even if your mate remains antagonistic to the Lord, you will experience a new level of spiritual growth and maturity.

Ways to help your mate. This is a difficult situation for both of you. Regardless of whether you like them or not, accept your mate's feelings.

"People don't change by being put down or evaluated. People change by being accepted ... judgment does not change people. Take off the black robe and get out of the role of a judge. Deal with what is, rather than what ought to be. Work toward acceptance rather than approval. Be beside the other person rather than on top of him. Acceptance is a suspension of judgment."[5]

Make your LifeMate the number one human being in your life. Reassure your LifeMate that your relationship is still top priority. To make this commitment come alive, let your mate have input on how your time together is spent. That will give your mate a feeling of security in the midst of change. Encourage your wife or husband to do something new that perhaps has always been a special dream. Take particular care of your sex life. It will be a powerful way to demonstrate your unconditional love for your LifeMate.

The best way to help your mate understand your love is to verbalize it to him or her. Keep quiet about your faith unless asked; yet live out the fruit of the Spirit before your LifeMate. If asked, be ready to lovingly share your faith. Pray for your special person and for yourself.

Ways to help yourself. You need a Christ-centered, positive support group or mentor. The majestic redwoods, found in Northern California, have a very shallow root system. It doesn't take much of a storm to topple them—unless they are growing in groves. In the midst of ferocious storms, they stand tall because their root systems have intertwined. As our lives intertwine with positive, Christ-centered people, we stand tall in the midst of difficult times.

How we relate to each other, affects our relationship with God. How we relate to God affects our marriage.

We received a letter from a most courageous woman who found herself unequally yoked. In the letter she shared that her first positive step had been to quit focusing on her husband and his faults and to begin facing areas where she needed personal growth. Then she flooded her mind with Scripture, using a planned memory system. Prayer and daily quiet times are a part of her spiritual disciplines. She shared with us that she is in a support group with other women who have non-Christian or unsupportive husbands. Together, these incredible women have created some guidelines for their support group. We think they're fantastic.

1. *Focus on the good.* Love your LifeMate as your partner, not your project! Dwell on things of good report (Phil. 4:8). Cling to what is good (Rom. 12:9).

2. *Resist the temptation to talk about your spouse.* Respect your husband (Eph. 5:33).

3. *Be more focused on what you can do rather than what your spouse is doing or not doing.* Give your LifeMate the grace that God gives you! Each of us will give an account of herself before God (Rom. 14:12).

4. *Each day, try to commit to do some definite action for your LifeMate.* Nail

down exactly what you are going to do. How? When? Then report back to your support group when it is done (Matt. 7:24–27 and James 1:22–25).

5. *Keep as your guide* 1 Corinthians 13:4–5: "Love is patient, love is kind. It does not envy, it does not boast, it is not proud. It is not rude, it is not self-seeking, it is not easily angered, it keeps no record of wrongs."

6. *No person will ever be able to meet the deep longing of your heart.* Only God can do that (1 Thess. 2:4, 6; Col. 3:23; 1 Cor. 15:58; Heb. 6:10).

The words of this unequally yoked woman speak for themselves: "I can't begin to tell you the transformation in my life. Circumstances haven't changed (yet!), but God has changed my heart toward the circumstances." We ask you, can you do without such a support group if your mate doesn't share your enthusiasm for the Lord? If you find yourself in this place, we highly recommend Lee and Leslie Strobel's book, *Surviving a Spiritual Mismatch*.

The Holy Spirit desires to live his power through us. Christ calls each of us to be Christ's feet, arms, hands, legs, smile, ears, and eyes to those special people we married. We are called to be God's love connection, but that is only possible if God is making his character traits a reality in our individual lives. Our emphasis doesn't need to be on whether we married the "right" partner; it needs to be whether, by the Holy Spirit's power, we are becoming the "right" partner.

How do you fill up your spirit? It is the filling up of your spirit in the good times that gives you the depth and breadth to handle the many challenges and curve balls of life.

Heart2Heart

1. Do you remember having questions about God and about faith as a child or as a teen? What were they? Who gave you answers?

2. Who had the most impact on your faith when you were a child? How did this person influence you?

3. If Scripture memorization was part of your upbringing, which is your favorite verse?

How do you build stillness and peace into your life? You and your LifeMate are "heirs together" of the grace of God. The Scriptures point out the interconnectedness of our marital and spiritual lives. First Peter 3:7 states that if a husband does not live in a considerate way with his wife, giving her respect as a fellow Christian, his prayers may be hindered. How we relate to each other affects our relationship with God. How we relate to God affects our marriage.

> Sometimes we must be willing to get rid of the life we expected, so as to experience the life that is waiting for us!

It seems as if we don't have to try terribly hard to come up with excuses for not growing together spiritually. We have three major forces pressuring us not to grow: the world, the flesh, and the devil. It seems to be easiest for us to succumb to the world's pressure by over-scheduling our calendars. There is barely time to sleep, let alone to study. Our flesh fights us with attitudes of laziness, pessimism, and shallowness. Then there is Satan's pressure. In James 4:7–8 we are told to resist the devil if we are going to draw near to God. Be aware of your enemies and control them, rather than letting them control you.

When loving God is our orienting principle, we are always adjusting to what God requires of us. That can't help but benefit our marriage.

You, Your LifeMate, and Scripture

In the beginning, God's Word called marriage into being. Now the Scriptures are crucial to our marriages. When a man and woman mutually agree to make Christ and God's Word central in their individual lives and also in their marriage, they begin to experience a marital transformation. The Scriptures become a daily guide to help develop the life pattern that will work for them. Their goal becomes a style of living that reflects Christ and thus produces satisfaction for both of them.

In good times, Scripture enriches our individual and shared lives. In difficult times, it both supports and challenges us. In times of conflict, it reminds us that the issue must be resolved or it will undermine our relationship. In betrayal times it rebukes us and challenges us to begin again.

Scripture Reading Ideas

1. Charlie and Martha Shedd have what they call a mutual "self-analysis" time. They read the same section of a book of the Bible separately. As they are reading, they put marks in the margins:

   Candle: "A new thought …"

   Arrow: "That hit me …"

   Question Mark: "I don't quite understand this …"

   Then they get together at an agreed-upon time and discuss it.

2. Read a devotional book using the tools of mutual "self-analysis."

3. Keep a journal separately. What is God saying to you through your personal study of his Word? Share it with each other once a week.

4. Discuss the implications of the weekend's sermon in your life and in your marriage.

5. Meditate on Psalm 34:1: "… his praise will always be on my lips." Cultivate an attitude of praise, positiveness, and enthusiasm.

6. Meditate in the same room over the same passage of Scripture. Try to picture it, hear it, smell it, and feel it. Then share your separate experiences with each other. "Be still and know that I am God" (Ps. 46:10).

7. Take advantage of seminars, lectures, and outstanding movies and books.

8. Collect Christian music that ministers to the two of you.

You, Your LifeMate, and Prayer

Pray together. Resist the temptation to protect yourselves from each other. Rather, lift one another up to the Lord at all times. When we pray for each other and show concern for each other's spiritual growth, we are demonstrating powerfully that we love. God is a master heart changer. Let down your guard. Be real with God and with each other.

1. Prayerwalking: Walking with Purpose

   Abraham walked with God. Noah walked with God. Enoch walked with God. What might happen if you and your LifeMate walked together with God?

   Today prayerwalking has become a popular trend, but more than twenty years ago when Charles and I started, I'd never heard of it. There was no mystery to it. We just did what we'd been doing—walking. … We just talked and then prayed about whatever we talked about. For example, I might mention a concern I had with one of our children or with my mother or a colleague. As soon as I voiced it, Charles would pray on the spot. If he shared a dilemma, I'd pray aloud for that. Then we'd take turns praying for our families, our church, friends, neighbors, etc.[6]

   Suggestion: Stop for coffee or enjoy breakfast at the end of your walk.

2. Are you uncomfortable praying? Share your prayer requests verbally with each other and then pray silently, holding hands.

3. Dave sometimes shares his prayer requests, and then I pray for him. Then we switch. This is most effective when the issue to be prayed about is hurtful.

4. Read prayers out loud to God.

5. Pray through the Psalms. Paraphrase King David's praises.

6. Keep a prayer journal together. Write out your prayers and God's answers to those prayers.

7. Set up a prayer calendar so you can make it through all of your prayer requests every week.

8. When your feelings are hurt, pray about it, and then ask yourself how your mate might be hurting. Thank God that he has forgiven you for (list specifics), and affirm that God meets your needs. Be honest with your mate. Apologize if necessary.

9. Once a week meet together and pray over each other's calendars. Ask

yourselves what kind of a husband or wife you've been during the past week. Ask God's help for the coming week. Our favorite time to do this is Sunday evening. It was especially helpful when our children were young.

10. Pray specifically for your LifeMate's contentment, peace of mind, wisdom in decision making, self-control, and relationships.

11. Prayer helps us to be obedient together.

My husband and I try to maintain an early morning time of prayer, and we've been more or less consistent. In warmer weather we like our patio, in winter we settle down in the living room, feeling snug as we look out at the cold weather. We commit the day and each other to God. Usually we pray through a list of concerns, needs, confessions and praises—always praises. It's hard at times not to feel perfunctory about this, as if we're quickly discharging a morning duty: brush teeth, shave, pray.

But "duty" isn't always a dirty word. Our prayer time gives us a refreshing pause in the morning rush; yet it has little to do, really, with what's good for us. It has everything to do with an old-fashioned word we don't hear much any more: obedience.[7]

> Religion is for those who are afraid to go to Hell, Spirituality is for those who have been there.

12. Devote ten minutes a day to silence for two weeks. During this time be absolutely still. Listen to hear the promptings from the Holy Spirit. Just sit and receive. After the ten minutes are up, write in your journal about what that was like for you.

13. Go away together on a silent retreat for one day once a year.

14. Move beyond the two-dimensional "Jesus and me" mentality, and be transformed by faith to a generous inclusiveness that seeks to serve. Pray together for a couple who doesn't yet know the Lord or who is

going through a separation or divorce. Support them and love them through your actions.

15. Disciple small groups separately. Come together and share the wonder of what the Lord is doing and what you're learning.

16. Develop a covenant relationship with one other couple.
    • Be willing to admit pain, need, and hurts.
    • Provoke one another to good works.
    • Inspire each other.
    • Hold each other accountable to grow.

17. Schedule an occasional weekend away to be together before the Lord. Work through your goals for your marriage, your children, and yourselves. Talk about how you can help each other achieve the desired goals.

18. Sing hymns and praise choruses together. Play an instrument. Dave plays the violin and I the piano—for our own amazement and each other's amusement. Our praise time is enriched by this.

19. Take advantage of informal opportunities to share Jesus with each other—times when you are both in the car, going for a walk, doing errands, hiking, and so forth. God is closer to you than even your problems.

Rate yourself on the following scale in reference to your level of spiritual connection. Where do you see yourself on this continuum? Share with your LifeMate.

Red Zone	Yellow Zone	Green Zone
I want nothing to do with Christianity.	My Christianity has become routine.	My faith in Christ is a priority and provides meaning.

Only as we are personally growing in our communion with Jesus Christ and drinking deeply and consistently of his love and acceptance, can we give to the person we live with. To give a gift freely, one must feel given to. Once again, we must affirm that this is only possible if Christ, not our LifeMate, or self, has first place in our life.

Truly, love merges us, enlarges us, and urges us to serve. All these suggestions are not to put you under condemnation. They are not suggested to add yet another "should" to your life. They are ways that together and separately you could commune with God.

Heart2Heart

1. Which of the above ideas do you think might work for you personally?

2. Which might work for you as a couple?

3. I feel most comfortable praying with you when …

Week 1: Pillow Talk

In your own life how would you like to see God more clearly? How would you like to love God more dearly? How would you like to follow him more nearly?

Week 2: Pillow Talk

How are you doing in expressing your personal faith as a living reality in front of your kids? How and when can you pray for your children's spiritual growth, their future, their relationships and their potential mates?

Week 3: Pillow Talk

Who in your life is a fantastic listener?

Who brings out the best in you?

Who encourages you when you're going through a tough time?

Who has acted as a mentor at various stages in your life?

Who points you to Jesus?

Who is a calming force in your life?

Who is a peacemaker?

Who are you open to taking confrontation from?

Who can you count on to be your prayer partner?

Who encourages the child in you to play and have fun?

Who is a compassionate person in your life?

Who has a faith that inspires you?

Who has sacrificed for you?

Week 4: Pillow Talk

One of the secrets of contentment is to focus on what we have left, not on what we have lost. What are the small gifts of simple existence that make you grateful to be alive? Create a fifty-item blessing list. Embrace the joys and blessings that are part of your life.

FROM PREVIOUS MONTH:

I COMMIT ON A DAILY BASIS TO BE A TEAM

PLAYER IN OUR RELATIONSHIP.

IN MY DESIRE TO LIVE ONE GOOD YEAR OF MARRIAGE WITH MY LIFEMATE,

I COMMIT TO MAKING MY SPIRITUAL RELATIONSHIP MY HIGHEST PRIORITY.

MONTH

TEN

"Sexuality: Leaving Behind Monotony"

> *"After fifteen years of marriage, they finally achieved sexual compatibility. They both had a headache!"*
>
> **Henry Ward Beecher[1]**

CONNECTING SEXUALLY IS THE BEST WAY to ensure a strong emotional and spiritual bond with your LifeMate. Like the grease that keeps a machine effectively running, sexual intimacy lubricates a marriage and each partner in the marriage. Among other benefits, a healthy, habitual and heartfelt intimate connection makes each LifeMate feel valued and appreciated. It relaxes us and reduces anxiety. It reassures us of our LifeMate's love and devotion and helps us to feel attractive.

Learning how to be lovers is a big deal. It's much more than just a physical act. It's about connection, intimacy, closeness, and affection. It's about being male and female. It's about becoming one.

Healthy sexuality connects a woman with her femininity. It awakens her sexuality, enhances her self-esteem, and increases her attraction to her husband. It helps her maintain higher estrogen levels, which lead to a better cardiovascular health and an overall feeling of well-being.

Healthy sexuality raises a man's testosterone level, which increases his confidence, vitality, strength, and energy. It awakens his masculinity, opens him up to his feelings, and reduces friction in the marriage. It increases his awareness of and attraction to his LifeMate. In addition, it sets him free to dream new goals and try new things, secure in his wife's love. We regain a part of ourselves when we choose to regain our sexuality!

Trust is the environment in which a healthy intimacy thrives—a trust that our LifeMates are both emotionally and physically available, a trust that when we turn in his or her direction we will find love, acceptance, comfort, and support as well as honesty, openness, and flexibility. Over time, your LifeMate becomes a trusted source of comfort and security, a secure base, and a haven of safety. After all, it is in the shelter of each other that we grow.

Do you love your LifeMate as they want to be loved or as you want to be loved?

When sex is used destructively in a marriage it is both the consequence of and the creation of a spiritual problem, a void within us and our relationship. When sexuality is a healthy natural part of an intimate connection, it is an integral part of the whole relationship. Imagine looking through a kaleidoscope at all the color particles used to create a mandola.[1] Imagine each color representing a facet of your life. One color represents your LifeMate, another your family, another your friends, another your work, another your hobbies, and another is your sexual relationship. As you turn the kaleidoscope, the particles change, constantly recreating the design. Sexuality is simply a part of life, sometimes more in the forefront than other parts, and sometimes in the background. It provides color and beauty. It is neither a devil nor a god. It is a wonderful part of an intimate marital relationship.

The Struggling Couple

Richie and Melissa loved each other deeply. They were committed to their marriage, their three kids, and to each other. Behind the closed doors of their bedroom, they were both suffering from incredible pain.

Richie was feeling rejected and angry because it felt to him like every time he initiated sex, he got shot down. Melissa felt pressure, intense pressure, yet in order for her to be in the mood she knew that she needed to feel emotionally connected, and most of the time she didn't feel that. In fact, anytime Richie would touch her, she would freeze up. She was afraid to respond to any of her husband's affectionate advances for fear that she'd have to have sex.

Richie was particularly upset that she didn't even respond to his affection. He was a sensitive, caring husband who made efforts in the romantic area and who tried to emotionally connect with his wife. His perspective was that no matter how sensitive he tried to be, she still perceived him as a sex-crazed, drooling animal.

After a period of time with no affection or sexual intimacy, Richie got more and more upset, sulky, and passionless. He felt like a robot going thorough the motions of life devoid of any emotion.

Melissa started to feel guilty and pressured for being a bad, unloving wife. She reached out and hugged him—then there was no stopping him. She went to bed with him and tried not to be a dead fish. At some point she felt a few pangs of desire; after all she knows that if she goes along for the ride, he'll be happier, less angry, and he'll back off and not pressure her for a while. This area of their relationship caused them both pain, panic, and pressure. It certainly didn't feel like a good gift from God. They found themselves gridlocked. The problem wouldn't go away, and their repeated arguments got them nowhere. What were they to do?

Heart**2**Heart

1. Has there been a time in your relationship that you could relate to either Richie or Melissa or both? Be specific.

2. Over the years of your marriage what do you think has led to a sexual mismatch?

3. How would you like to improve this area of your relationship?

From Jan and Dave's Journal:

Ten years into our marriage, we attended one of Cliff and Joyce Penner's weekend retreats. It was outstanding. Together they have written The Gift of Sex: A Christian Guide to Sexual Fulfillment.[2] *We recommend this and any of their other books.*

At the seminar, we were given a homework assignment. It was one of the most difficult and freeing things for us personally. We recommend it highly. The assignment was to stand in front of a full-length mirror stark naked. Your partner was to sit on the bed and be completely still. You were to talk about your feelings about every part of your body, including the genitals. Start at the top of your head and work down to your toes.

What do you like? What don't you like? When you were finished talking, your husband or wife was to tell you how he or she felt about your body. You were to listen and accept. Together then, you were to thank God for the wonder of his creation.

Talk about anxiety. This was the first time in our marriage that we broke through the sexual sound barrier. Up to this point in time we had made love in ways that ensured that neither of us would be too anxious. When we started to talk honestly about our satisfactions and dissatisfactions, we began to move into unfamiliar territory. We learned that we had to tolerate anxiety before it goes away, that our separate and mutual anxieties had limited our sexual relationship, and that we needed to stretch out of our sexual comfort zone in order to be comfortable and satisfied later. We learned that working separately to reduce our own anxiety ultimately worked incredibly in our relationship.

Transition Toward a Satisfying, Sensual, and Spiritual Sexuality

Lord, help us find those places in us which we have never opened to your love. Show us the subterranean chambers we have forgotten, the dark rooms where some small part of us is hiding. These too we hope to share—the musty and the moldy, the decayed and the rancid. Cleanse us that we might more fully uncover all of us, known and unknown. Beginning now, lead us toward a total relationship with each other and with you.[3]

God wants you to enjoy sex! It is a gift created by the same tender Savior who loved each of us enough to give us the ultimate gift of himself.

Love is God's absolute bottom line. In fact, God is love. The closer we get to this kind of a God—the more we learn to "let go"—the greater the possibility of drawing closer to our mate.

Our mutual expressions of love can be a taste of the divine on earth, if we agree that sex is one of God's good and perfect gifts. After God created male and female, he said:

"And it was very good" (Gen. 1:31).

"So God made man like his Maker: Like God did God make man; Man and maid did he make them....Then God looked over all that he had made, and it was excellent in every way" (Gen. 1:27, 31 TLB).

According to Scripture, sexuality in marriage is for mutual benefit, to promote enjoyment, to provide connection and closeness, and to produce children. The bottom line scripturally is that God wants us to open up and to trust that physical intimacy is a good gift from him.

That's mighty different from the "I'll just do my duty but don't expect me to enjoy it" or the "men are just animals" attitude. We're so glad it's different in our marriage. Let's allow the inner presence of the Holy Spirit to free us up to increasingly enjoy what God has approved of completely.

Address Your Reality

Just as it is not normal to feel in love with your LifeMate constantly, it is also not normal to feel sexually attracted to him or her all the time.

Heart2Heart

1. Circle the words that describe how you perceive sex.

Life-affirming celebration	Dishonesty and shame
Emotional isolation	Mutual respect
Caring	Enhanced self-esteem
Open communication	Limited options
Betrayal of trust	Imbalance of power
Coercion and fear	Emotional intimacy
Risk and danger	Healthy bonding
Sense of equality	Silencing of own inner reality
Impulsive, compulsive	Dislike of partner
Disintegration of relationship	Consent
Trust	Pain and injury
Creative expression	Safety

2. Children learn so much from their parents' marriage. What did you experience in your home growing up that shaped your perspective about your body, about sexuality, and about being a man or a woman?

3. What did you learn and experience as an adolescent and as an adult that shaped your perspective about your appearance, your body, your sexuality, and your gender?

Complete the following sentences and discuss with each other.

1. The best thing about our sex life is …

2. My father left me with this impression about sex …

3. My mother left me with this impression about sex …

4. Prior to our marriage I felt sex was …

5. I find you sexually attractive in these ways …

6. One time I particularly appreciated a romantic gesture you made was …

7. I find it difficult to initiate sexually when …

8. When I initiate sexually I feel …

9. I am most excited by you when …

10. When we have gone a week without any sexual intimacy I feel …

11. I feel sexually frustrated when …

12. A sexual fantasy I have involving you is …

13. My favorite time to make love is …

14. I would like to try …

15. A sexual fear I have is …

16. I would like you to touch me in this way …

17. To me oral sex is …

18. When I initiate and you ignore it I feel …

19. I would like it if you approached me by …

20. If you are saying no to my advances I would like you to …

Just because you are experiencing a cloudy day does not mean that the sun has permanently disappeared; it's just temporarily covered. Desire fluctuates depending on multiple factors. Listed below is an extensive list of common causes of sexual difficulties. As you can see from the list, many factors, both physiological and psychological, affect our sexuality.

Common Causes of Sexual Difficulties!

- Family background. Sex is something you have to do because men need it, but don't expect any personal enjoyment.
- Family background. It was never spoken of. It was a taboo to bring up sex and talk about it. Sex isn't for nice girls.
- Cultural attitudes about sex that cause you to feel bad about yourself or shamed about your actions.
- Distorted religious beliefs. Sex is somehow shameful.
- Experiences of physical, emotional, or sexual abuse.
- Control issues that began in the early stages of dating. We learn to go only so far to keep our love new and interesting, but not so far

that we lose respect or become pregnant. We learn to be in our heads controlling our feelings rather than into the sexual experience. After doing this repeatedly for a period of time it is difficult to let go of the control we spent so long developing.

- Previous sexual experiences that haunt your bedroom.
- Communication problems: When you try to talk you experience your LifeMate's refusal to be influenced or to talk.
- Unresolved power struggles. It's difficult to make love when you can't make peace.
- Lack of forgiveness. An inability to let go of the bad feelings that usually accompany arguments. You keep score and hold grudges.
- Inability to forgive yourself for your sexual choices.
- Clinical depression. If so, your sexual interest is the first thing to go.
- Fertility Problems. Sex becomes goal-oriented and loses its tenderness.
- Illness or medications, including birth control.
- Hormonal imbalance.
- Side effects of chemotherapy.
- A lack of sexual knowledge.
- Emotional and physical fatigue. Just the thought of being sexual feels like a chore.
- Motherhood: Especially in the first year after having a baby.
- Boredom, which usually camouflages unconscious anger.
- Prolonged stress.
- Grief over an extreme loss personally, financially, and/or relationally.
- I am uncomfortable and even mortified at the idea of talking about our sexual relationship.
- I believe that my LifeMate is unsupportive of me and my feelings.
- A belief as a woman that submission means giving in and giving up. Therefore, as a woman I have no personal power. I must be dependent and helpless. If I don't believe that I have the power to

get what I need directly then I will get it indirectly through the power of withholding. Sex is a powerful thing to withhold.

- A belief as a man that a woman who talks clearly about what she wants and needs is controlling and demanding.
- A belief that sex is equal to intercourse. Sex is defined too narrowly.
- In the past my LifeMate asked me to do things that I found offensive and demeaning. I felt shame.
- In our relationship "no" is not welcomed.
- I hate my body, and I am constantly self-consciousness.
- I see my LifeMate as quite critical.
- My LifeMate is looking at pornography and involved in cyber-sex.
- One of us is in a midlife crisis and wondering about continued commitment after all life is passing us by.
- My LifeMate is a constant source of sexual pressure.
- I can't relax. Performance anxiety haunts me.
- I am turned off by my LifeMate's behavior. He or she may neglect cleanliness, has gained excessive weight or turned into a couch potato. He or she may be hostile, demanding, critical, or drunk in the bedroom. He or she may approach me in a crass, demeaning way.
- My LifeMate is a flirt with other people but not with me.
- I know that my LifeMate is attracted to or involved with someone else.
- One or both of us uses alcohol, tobacco, or illegal substances such as heroin, cocaine, or marijuana.
- My LifeMate takes on the position of amateur therapist and psychoanalyzes me and my sexual feelings and performance.

> We regain a part of ourselves when we choose to regain our sexuality!

- My LifeMate pulls out the Bible, especially 1 Corinthians 7:4, and condemns me and threatens me with it.
- We have gone so long without an intimate sexual relationship I don't feel any need for it.

Acquaint Yourself with Biology

Scientists now believe that when we are attracted to someone, when we "fall in love" and enter that fabulous stage of romantic love, our brain experiences a chemical change. Michael Liebowitz, a research psychiatrist refers to it as a "love cocktail." Phenylethylamine (PEA), a naturally occurring amphetamine-like neurotransmitter and several other excitatory neurotransmitters, including dopamine, create the ingredients for this cocktail. We are rendered maniacally optimistic about the person we love. The problem is that the brain cannot externally maintain this "high." It's as if over time lovers develop a tolerance for each other. Euphoria dwindles and reality descends. Usually this happens sometime within the first two years of marriage for those who have not been sexually active prior to marriage.

Often what is left in its place is a desire gap between LifeMates. This gap is caused by a second biological factor—testosterone. Both sexes produce this. Men manufacture testosterone in their testes and adrenals, women from their ovaries and adrenals. Women or men can have high or low testosterone levels. The levels drop gradually with age.

Because when we first meet, our brains are full of the aphrodisiac properties of PEA and other brain chemicals, we don't realize or even know that there is a disparity in libido. When reality sets in, the high-T LifeMate can feel tremendously disappointed. The low-T LifeMate often questions their sexual normalcy. He or she may even feel shame or deeply

---

Heart**2**Heart

1. Which of these difficulties have influenced your intimate relationship?

2. Why do you think these have been a challenge for you?

3. Would you benefit from having a thorough physical, from talking to physician (a gynecologist, an endocrinologist, or a urologist) or a therapist? Share your perspective with your LifeMate.

resent the other LifeMate's pressure to have sex when he or she feels little to no sexual desire.[4]

Knowing that this low sexual desire comes from a low testosterone level and is biologically based, not a result of a lack of attraction, a lack of care for the other, or a sign that we are no longer in love, is important. It is at this point that we need to commit to steady, vigilant efforts to sustain our intimate relationship. This requires both LifeMates to stretch beyond their respective sexual comfort zones. We must stretch to understand, to empathize with, and to accommodate our LifeMate's desires and wishes. This is yet another area in marriage where "iron must sharpen iron." After all, differences in hobbies, vacations, and food are accepted and even enjoyed. Why not make your marriage big enough for a desire discrepancy too?

Heart**2**Heart

1. Does the information above focused on brain chemistry affect in any way your expectations or your perspective about yourself or your LifeMate?

2. What would your LifeMate say you've been doing or saying lately in regard to your sexual differences that is absolutely driving him or her nuts? To do the same thing and expect different results is not too smart.

> Understanding how each partner's experience of passion can be both different from one's own and entirely valid can lead to a state of marital grace that I call mature love. Desire differences are natural and normal. Relax.[5]

Accept Your Body

We cannot have satisfying sex if we are uncomfortable with each other's bodies, visually and tactilely. Our enjoyment will be increased if we appreciate and accept our own bodies.

If we feel shame and self-consciousness when our partner's eyes look at us naked, it is enough to keep us from relaxing into our sexual feelings. Have you ever faced your uncomfortable feelings long enough to ask where they came from?

Three factors determine our body image: feedback, sensory input, and the models we mimic. What did you learn in childhood about the attractiveness of your body? The feedback could have come from peers, brothers or sisters, mother or dad, teachers, friends, or enemies. What nicknames were pinned on you? Many of us are prone to defining ourselves in the same way that a negative voice did in the past.

The amount of touching that you received in your home also affects your body image. Did you learn that you were indeed touchable? Did you learn that if you touched yourself, you would be cruelly and severely punished? If this was the case, it probably didn't take you long to realize that parts of your body were "bad." Did you learn that you had no right to your own body?

What models do you hold up as ideal? We live in a culture that says we have to earn our value by how we look. So we spend the vast majority of our time comparing ourself to others. The purpose of the billion-dollar cosmetic industry is to persuade us all that we need help— some a little and some a lot. What is the result? We grow up with insecurities. In this arena we compare our worst, of which we are most aware, with everyone else's best, which is all we ever see. What a negative impact this has on our sexual intimacy! It is a definite desire squelcher. Do you care enough about God, yourself, and your LifeMate to move against a negative body image? It is possible to choose to feel differently.

Facing Your Body Image.

1. *Get into God's Word.* We must not be ashamed to consider what God wasn't ashamed to create! What does God say about your body? Look up these verses:

    Psalm 139:14: I praise you because I am fearfully and wonderfully made; your works are wonderful, I know that full well.

    Proverbs 5:18–19: May your fountain be blessed, and may you rejoice in the wife of your youth. A loving doe, a graceful deer—may her breasts satisfy you always,

may you ever be captivated by her love.

Read the Song of Solomon in *The Message* paraphrase out loud to each other. There will be moments that you will probably feel uncomfortable with such straight forward, sensual, and playful conversation.

The wonder, awe, and excitement with which God views our bodies needs to be contrasted with the negative feedback you received as a child and that you are feeding on today. As an adult you must make a choice which voice you are going to meditate on. It's your decision.

2. *Get comfortable with your own body.* Most people who don't like their bodies rarely, if ever, look at them. Self-image often exists only in the imagination. Rare is the woman who is pleased with how her breasts look. The real problem is that they don't look the way they did on Barbie dolls, starlets, or "siliconized" playmates. We may be Christians, but we do live in this world, and its standards for beauty affect us. We can complain about our bodies so long that we finally convince ourselves and our mates that we are unattractive. Be wise.

    If you are grateful for the body God gave you, and if you are willing to look at its beauty, you will become attractive to yourself and then to your LifeMate. Get undressed and look yourself over, head to toe, in a full-length mirror. For once, focus on what you like about your body instead of what you don't like. All the while, talk to yourself, giving a running commentary on what you see; for example: "There is something soft and inviting about my neck, isn't there? No wonder he likes to snuggle there. ..." Or, for a man: "When I stand straight, my shoulders do have a strong, square look. Not bad." Don't miss a spot. Give yourself a real once-over.

    God created that body. It is wondrously made. It pleased him. Do you know what your genitals look like? Take the time to examine them in the mirror, too. Perhaps to your surprise, you will discover that they don't look "grotesque" or "dirty." God approved of them. Get familiar with how they really look. Sex begins with a relaxed appreciation of your own body.

3. *Exercise.* You just knew we'd say it, didn't you? Staying in shape physically is the main way we can stay in shape sexually. It is possible that you really are too tired for sex. Rest isn't the answer; exercise is.

We can't guarantee that you will live longer, but you will live with more enthusiasm, and you'll love better. Sex is a physical act. The most satisfying sex begins when we are completely relaxed. There is no more effective way to become relaxed and ready for love than physical exercise. Could you and your mate take a brisk walk each evening? Try to get your walking up to thirty minutes a day minimum.

4. Get lots of sensory experiences. Do you feel that every time your LifeMate touches you it will lead to intercourse? If so, this habit pattern must be broken. Touch is healing. There needs to be much touching of each other without demand. Do you snuggle up to your love when he or she is reading or watching TV? Let him or her know that touching is pleasure enough.

5. Pray together and separately. Praise and thank God for the marvelous gift he has given both of you. After you have enjoyed making love, don't turn over in bed like you're a big bump on a log or a hibernating bear. Hold each other tight and praise God for each other and the gift of sex. Perhaps then you can enjoy a bubble bath and touch and talk and pray and touch some more.

6. Affirm each other over and over and over again.

"You've got the greatest body."

"I desire your touch."

"You are so beautiful (handsome)."

Admit That Being Lovers Doesn't Come Naturally

The movies would have us believe that intercourse is instinctual and good sex comes naturally. If we believe that, we will be disappointed. What leads us to believe that all social, intellectual, and psychomotor behavior requires instruction, training, and practice, but sex does not? When talking to a group of husbands, Ed Wheat said, "If you do what comes naturally in lovemaking, you can count on being wrong almost 100 percent of the time."

Whatever you do, don't assume that if your LifeMate were a good lover he or she would just automatically know what you need. That is a romantic fantasy not grounded in reality. How are husbands supposed to know what makes a woman purr when they have never been a woman and vice versa? Be a student of your LifeMate!

Listed on the following page are the differing sexual needs of husbands and wives. As with any list of this kind, there will be exceptions. Study this list together and then let your LifeMate succeed in pleasing you.

Activate Your Willingness to Be an Initiator

Initiating sex is a conscious decision, not a sudden inspiration. The truth is, when we initiate we aren't feeling sexy, we are planning on it.

Because it is a conscious decision, we are really saying that we want sex. That admission, rather than bringing joy, has the potential to bring anxiety and external guilt to some. Perhaps your childhood instruction taught you that sex is dirty and bad, and you will be punished for enjoying it.

There are so many diversions in our culture. We can over-schedule; we can get involved in a TV program; we can be concerned about the children; we can be tired or sick; it can be too early or too late—or we may need more sleep.

If your husband has always initiated, he has never had the opportunity of experiencing sex as a demand, and you have never had sex because you wanted it.

In a power-hungry marriage, the husband uses sex to control his wife and she, in turn, refuses sex showing him who is really in charge. You need to relinquish the power and each initiate. This will give both of you

Heart2Heart

1. How different would your life and your energy be if you truly stopped worrying about and focusing on your imperfections? Be specific.

2. What can you change about your body? Make a list and prioritize it in areas of importance. Take this list to your support person and pray over it together. Then take specific actions steps on a daily basis to move you closer to your goal. Write these steps down where you will review them every day.

3. What can't you change or are you unwilling to change?

the feeling of being wanted. We recommend that you alternate the initiating just as you alternate your date nights.

DIFFERING SEXUAL NEEDS

WIFE	HUSBAND
Stimulated by touch and tender words all day long prior to sexual time.	Stimulated by visual first.
Needs love to open up to sex.	Needs sex to open up to love.
Needs to relax and get into sex slowly; lots of touching—thirty minutes.	Starts out all ready to go.
Great communication to enjoy sex.	Sex opens a man up to his feelings. Sex precedes communication.
Needs time to enjoy sex.	Needs an occasional "quickie."
Pleasure is increased by direct stimulation of non-erogenous zones first.	Pleasure is increased by direct stimulation of erogenous zones first.

To begin with, there needs to be much nondemanding touching. Encourage the more hesitant partner to initiate. Sexual arousal is a pleasure in itself. We would recommend that you continue to make it a nondemand experience until your bodies have made friends.

Nondemand pleasuring is pleasure-oriented touching for its own sake. Avoid intercourse until you both have relaxed and enjoyed multiple kinds of nondemand pleasuring. Value touching in and of itself.

Sexuality is meant to be a part of our life from birth to death. It is fueled by love, emotional maturity, comfort, attraction, and time; not by youth, newness, or physical beauty. Sex includes nondemand pleasuring:

kissing, body massage, taking showers and baths together, playful touching while clothed and semi-clothed, cuddling, dancing together, neck and back massages, caressing playful touch, and so forth. Even if you refrain from sex in its narrowest definition (intercourse) for a period of time, don't refrain from nondemand pleasuring. It will keep you intimately connected.

Sometimes one of you will not be in the mood for sex. Every sexual refusal does not have to be viewed as a rejection. Many people don't initiate sex anymore because they can't risk a rejection. Establish between the two of you that there is freedom to refuse and that it is not rejection. But remember that a sustained pattern of avoidance feeds on itself. In our marriage we have found it helps to set an alternative time to have an intimate date if we say no on a given day. Then we keep that date. Ask yourself, do you get pleasure by giving pleasure?

Heart2Heart

1. How does it impact you when your LifeMate initiates romantic actions and intimate connection?

2. Create a list of your favorite nondemand touching activities. Try them out and enjoy them.

3. How can we make it okay to say no in our relationship?

Week 1: Date Night

Create your own version of a drive-in by hitting your favorite local fast-food joint. Why don't you order burgers, fries, and milk shakes? Then take a ride to the most scenic area of your hometown. Park the car. Talk and enjoy your dinner. For dessert, try some good old-fashioned necking until you just have to go home.

Week 2: Date Night

Go shopping together for items that will go into your "I'm anticipating making love with you" basket" Perhaps you might choose a new CD that you both enjoy, some massage oil, bubble bath, candles, a special loofah sponge, chocolates, sparkling cider, goblets, a new item of lingerie and some new boxer shorts, and so on. Have an enchanted evening together.

Week 3: Date Night

Send your LifeMate an e-mail early in the week inviting him or her to an at-home private party. Farm the kids out. That evening turn your living room or family room into a romantic space by moving the coffee table off to the side. Lay down layers of soft blankets. Cover the lamps with scarves, light scented candles, and put fresh flowers in the room. Have lots of your favorite CDs, some snacks to nibble on, and some massage oil. Settle in for a wonderful, uninterrupted evening of enjoyment.

Week 4: Date Night

Hold a "his" or "her" night. Set it in motion by laying out a small mono-grammed towel if you have one. If your husband lays out the "hers" towel, he is in charge of planning a night that revolves entirely around his wife, from her favorite restaurant and entertainment to what she loves and enjoys in bed. If the wife lays out the "his" towel she plans an evening that revolves around her husband.

Go with it! The laundry can wait!

Rate yourself on the following scale in reference to your level of spiritual connection. Where do you see yourself on this continuum? Share with your LifeMate.

Red Zone	Yellow Zone	Green Zone
Conflictual Team Sex causes pain & distrust in our relationship. When my LifeMate walks into a room I walk out.	Evolving Team We are in process. We are talking & touching more. It gives us both pleasure. When my LifeMate walks into a room I acknowledge him or her.	We enjoy our intimate relationship. When my LifeMate walks into a room I beam inside thinking, "This is my man." "This is my woman."

FROM PREVIOUS MONTH:

I COMMIT TO MAKING OUR SPIRITUAL
RELATIONSHIP MY HIGHEST PRIORITY.

**IN MY DESIRE TO LIVE ONE GOOD YEAR
OF MARRIAGE WITH MY LIFEMATE,**

I COMMIT TO MAKING OUR SEXUAL
RELATIONSHIP SATISFYING, SENSUAL,
AND SPIRITUAL.

MONTH

ELEVEN

"Balance: Leaving Behind Instability"

> "Life is not a stress rehearsal"

HOW OFTEN DO YOU GO THROUGH THE day feeling tilted to one side? You're busy all day long, but strangely unsatisfied. Are you living off-center? What is at the center of your life?

When we take care of what is at our center and then live out of our center, life takes on purpose, our pursuits are fulfilling, and we feel a deep sense of significance. We pay attention to ourselves, to others, and face life more deliberately. Change and challenges don't derail us. We live directed by an internal compass rather than driven by multiple external compulsions. We are anchored, as it were, in our soul. As a result we see ourselves, the people in our life, the work of our hands, and the way we spend our time differently. We live in the present, rather than agonizing over the past or living in a state of perpetual panic about the future.

Even if you win the rat race, you are still a rat!

Lilly Tomlin
(Goodman, Joel; Laffirmations, Health Communications, Deerfield Beach, Florida, p.XIV

A Balanced Couple

One Christmas we received a treasure of a Christmas letter from some precious friends, Kate and Jeff. We were deeply touched by the way they embraced the stage of life in which they found themselves and by the rhythm of balance they had discovered. It obviously brought joy to the two of them. With their permission, we share portions of their letter with you.

"Greetings, Dear Friends:

We hope you had a meaningful, nourishing Christmas. We delayed our letter this year in order to simplify our holiday preparations. So here's the year in review. 2002 was "nice." And in a quiet, important way it was family life that defined it best. Kristofer took swimming and Kindermusik, became mostly potty trained, moved into a 'big boy' bed, turned two, and constantly delighted us with songs, rhymes, and silliness. The big event for us was our tenth anniversary, which we celebrated for eleven days in the Maritimes of Canada. ... Throughout the year we enjoyed birthday parties with cousins, trips to Kate's family farm, and a visit from our Scandinavian friends. In the summer, Jeff traveled the province (Saskatchewan, Canada) working on tourism photo shoots. This included a swim down Otter Rapids. He still insists that it's work that he does. Kate taught music, tended a fruitful garden, sewed a beautiful quilt for Kristofer, and managed the household. ... Somewhere in there we found out that

Kristofer was expecting a younger sibling, due late March. … We both continued to lead in various ways at our church, from nursery and personnel to strategic planning and music. In between was a lot of stuff, called day-to-day. And so we feel like we're settling down in some ways and discovering profound meaning in bubble bath, the alphabet, and Franklin the turtle. We are grateful for our family and friends, gifts of God to us … We trust that you will find meaning and joy in this year ahead, through the highs and lows, and that you may find the One True Friend walking close beside you. Have fun! Try something new. And make time for who you love and what you love to do."

From Jan's Journal:

As I write this chapter on balance I face a personal reality. I have never achieved a perfect balance in life. Balance seems an elusive, slippery slope in my life. I certainly know that if I try to live up to our culture's definition of what a woman "should" be able to accomplish (unfortunately that applies to our Christian culture, too), I will fail. I will be left a bundle of nerves with a short fuse, feeling a daily sense of inadequacy. Living life from the outside in always has that impact on me.

I often feel like I have one foot up in the air trying not to be blown over by the next gust of wind. This year I celebrated our daughter's wedding, wrote two books, ministered through my full-time counseling responsibilities, and continued to develop, with our capable support team, the ministry known as LifeMates. Frankly, at times it's probably seemed insane to those near and dear to me. Yet to me, even though at times life

Heart2Heart

1. What were the different aspects of life Kate and Jeff were attempting to balance?

2. Without even knowing Kate and Jeff, what values would you say they operate from?

3. What do you think needs to change in your personal or married life in order to establish balance?

was crazy busy, I have been living out of my deepest values, desires, hopes, and dreams. That has felt deeply fulfilling. There has been satisfaction in spite of my imbalance.

I have to confess, for the first time in my life I had to phone our publisher and request an extension in deadline. They graciously granted it. I am looking forward to uninterrupted down time with Dave after the deadline for this book is met.

Marriage provides an opportunity to make one person feel wanted and special throughout their lifetime!

Over the years I have learned that balance doesn't mean that all the balls of my life are up in the air in perfect balance. It means that I am operating out of my value system. I welcome God into my day, and enjoy him throughout my day. I celebrate and create space for love and relationship, I am challenged by hard work, and I make time for exercise. When I embrace that value system, I can celebrate a wonderfully interesting unbalanced life.

Transition Toward Balance

A life without stress would be dull and stagnant. A life with too much stress is overwhelming, depressing, and dangerous. Up to a point stress helps us think, cope, and work better. Past that point, stress tears us up. We all need to find a place of equilibrium where we have stress without distress. Unfortunately many of us have only experienced distress.

Sometimes we find ourselves running so fast that there is no time to sit down and figure out where we are headed. Time, like money, needs to be accounted for. Have you ever noticed how quickly money can disappear? The cup of Starbuck's® coffee, a quick lunch with friends, a trip to the drug store, and your wallet is empty. The same is true of time. Unless we prioritize it, it just disappears without even a whimper. Time is a gift that is easy to take for granted.

We all get the same amount of time: 168 hours a week, 52 weeks a year. If we assume that work takes up 55 hours a week (including time spent at the office, commuting time, which in California could add 10 hours to your week, time spent preparing for work and worrying about work) and 50 hours for sleeping, all that remains is 63 hours for everything else. These numbers don't even take into account the 24-hour-a-day job of parenting children, if you happen to be a parent.

Periodically every couple needs to ask this question: "Is our life polluting our marriage?"

Life is polluting your marriage if at the end of the day you have nothing left for each other, if

Heart2Heart

Where does your time go? Make a chart like the one below on separate paper, and keep track of how you spend your time for one week. Be aware of the amount of time you really spend with each other on any given day.

What did you learn as a result of doing this exercise? How was the majority of your time spent? Has your life been polluting your relationship?

Day	Minutes We Spent Together	Activities Shared
Monday		
Tuesday		
Wednesday		
Thursday		
Friday		
Saturday		
Sunday		

impatience and anger are your primary emotions, if everything about your LifeMate starts to irritate you, if you find yourself avoiding your LifeMate, if you don't want to help your LifeMate in any practical ways, and if life is all about you.

Has stress become your sanctuary? Are you hooked on speed? Do your thoughts run 1,000 miles an hour, and do your actions echo your racing thoughts?

In times of stress, epinephrine, norepinephrine, glucocorticoids, and cortical are all manufactured in our body. When we're high on stress we're less aware of our own pain and the pain we're causing in other's lives.

Unfortunately stress hormones have side effects that can kill us. Over time, they contribute to ulcers and heart disease, they weaken the immune system, cortisol creates a craving for carbohydrates and leaves us vulnerable to everything from depression to accidents. These physical side effects don't even take into account the relational side effects in the lives of the people we run over. We keep the high going by exacerbating or creating incidents that result in intense anger and fear.

If you are reading this section and feeling as if it doesn't apply, ask yourself these questions:

1. When was the last time I procrastinated?
2. When was the last time my tendency toward perfectionism created problems for me or for my LifeMate?
3. When was the last time I obsessed about my obligations?
4. When was the last time I said yes when my insides were screaming no?
5. When was the last time I let my imagination loose on worst case scenarios?
6. Do I have significant relationships in which people brood or worry a great deal?
7. When was the last time I over-generalized, "catastrophized," personalized, and viewed life pessimistically? What effect has this had on my stress level and on my life?

It isn't until we realize that time is limited and that we have choices that we really consider how we spend our time. When we become aware, the words yes and no become powerful words and become examples of stewardship.

Heart2Heart

1. Write down the top five priorities that need your focus for the next six months. What personal values do each of these priorities represent?

2. In order for those five priorities to be important, other things may need to be put aside. What things will you have to let go of, or give very little attention to over the next six months?

3. What is one action step per day or per week (whichever time frame is appropriate for you), that could move you toward your priority? List actions on your calendar or enter them on your computer or personal electronic organizer.

4. Use the circle below. Divide it into eight equal sections. Give each piece of the pie a different label: spiritual life, marriage, family, health and exercise, work, ministry and community involvement, personal renewal, and friends.

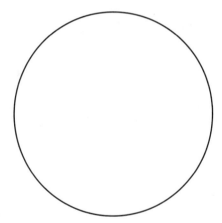

Use two different colored pens. Each of you place a dot in each section marking the degree to which you feel satisfied in that particular area: a dot near the outer rim means you are very satisfied; one placed near the center indicates that you are not satisfied with that area. Now connect the dots and take a good look. Does it seem lopsided? Perhaps there are areas of the pie that you have ignored or neglected. You have the power to change that.

What did you learn from this exercise? Is there something missing in your life?

An important part of balance is to know when to stop struggling.

Herbert Benson, MD and William Proctor have written a thought-provoking book called, *The Break Out Principle*.[1] The "break out principle" happens when you are striving toward some goal but you get frustrated, stuck, irritated, and exhausted. Their thesis is, when you reach that point, instead of pushing harder, you let go. That's the time to turn to some completely different activity. It helps if it is something mindless and repetitive to get your mind off the struggle. It might be as mundane as shaving or folding clothes or going for a bike ride. Often when we are focused on this mindless task, the solution to the problem comes to us. That is breakout! Dr. Benson and Mr. Proctor suggest that once we understand this concept we can actively make it happen in our lives whenever we get stuck. Might this also apply to marriage? Perhaps we'd do better to call a time-out if we're in a dead-end argument, go for a walk, or do a mundane task and then return to our discussion later. What do you think?

A renowned filmmaker and artist helped teach a fellow psychologist about balance. The psychologist who was helped said this about his friend.

> When he works he becomes totally absorbed in his work, but he always leaves room for play. In fact, nothing—and I mean nothing—gets in the way of his play. His playtime enriches his life as much as any artistic achievement or outside honor bestowed upon him, probably more. It gives him something to look forward to with enthusiasm regularly, and it lets him return to his work with renewed energy.
>
> He sets high goals and pursues them vigorously, but on a day-to-day basis he does not fail to appreciate his family, his own accomplishments, and the people around him. I love going to his house to ask if the "old man" can come out to play. He appreciates

each experience so much that he's a delight to be with. His enthusiasm and vitality rub off on all those around him.

He used to accuse me jokingly of sitting at home writing books about having fun while he was out doing it. I reflected on the way he had come to keep playfulness at the center of a life that otherwise revolves around perfection and the pursuit of excellence. A near fatal heart attack, which almost grabbed his life, helped teach him this lesson. He was thankful for another day of living ... then another, and another. So many days to live and experience and enjoy. A gift of life![2]

Leaving your desk may be an investment in the quality of your life!

When You Want More Time Together!

Once upon a time the two of you couldn't wait to be together. Work was what you did in between being together. Perhaps today work has become a comfortable refuge from each other. After all, work offers tangible results. The report is done, the meeting was successful, you land the contract, or you get a raise. The payoffs of a personal life are more difficult to measure. They are timeless: a feeling of fulfillment, balance, energy, and love. If you want to make more time for the two of you, consider the following possibilities:

1. Cut down on TV watching. Never watch a rerun. Don't consider time spent watching TV as spending time together unless you cuddle and talk to each other about what you are watching.

2. Schedule fifteen to thirty minutes a day to share a beverage and catch up on the good things that happened in one another's day.

3. Once a week schedule an hour to work through issues that have raised their heads and need to be resolved. Each of you gets thirty minutes and no more. You can always schedule time on another day

if necessary. We always schedule our discussion prior to 9:00 p.m. for obvious reasons.

4. Schedule a date time once a week.
5. Schedule separate time. Encourage and do your best to facilitate your LifeMate's time.
6. Schedule times of physical intimacy.
7. Schedule a day of rest.
8. Hire people to perform time-consuming chores.
9. Kiss perfectionism good-bye. Relax your standards to "good enough."
10. Buy less. Shopping can be time-consuming.
11. Discover something you both enjoy doing and do it regularly: exercise, bike riding, hiking, visiting galleries or museums, playing musical instruments, and so on.
12. Worship together and separately.
13. Intentionally notice and affirm your LifeMate for appearance, effort, personality, and/or character on a regular basis.
14. Once a week help with something that isn't on your chore list.
15. Spend less time socializing with people who drain you.

What Drains Me?

Whenever we direct our thoughts toward balance, we need to face those things in our life that keep us in a state of instability.

Make a list of things, which if eliminated from your life, would instantly give you a sense of relief. (Things like organizing your desk, sorting through your closet, paying off a debt, making a phone call that you dread, getting off a committee, etc.)

Do you need to ask for help so that you are not carrying a heavy load totally alone (sick child, aging parent, housekeeping, etc)?

Take what you learned by answering these two questions to your support people. Together, figure out how to remove the top three energy drainers in your life. Break your plan into small steps. Only tackle one energy drainer at a time. It might mean spending thirty minutes a day sorting papers. When you take care of one energy drainer, reward yourself. Then do the same thing for the next energy drainer.

What Renews Me?

The last time you were on an airplane did you hear the flight attendant suggest that if you are traveling with a young child, you are to put your personal oxygen mask on first and the child's on next? When we put the needs of everyone else and the demands of our business before our own needs, we are entering a danger zone. If our sense of adequacy depends on other people being pleased with us, having everyone like and approve of us, doing everything perfectly and being "top dog," our life will be out of balance.

We all need moments when we come back to our centers for rejuvenation. We call these "oxygen mask moments." If we neglect to recharge a battery, it will die. If we run full speed ahead, we lose momentum to finish our race, and yet many of us don't make personal renewal much of a priority. We have found that it is the filling up of our spirit in the good times that gives us the depth and breadth to handle the tough times.

Here are some suggestions of activities and questions that if taken seriously could improve the quality of your life. Ask yourselves:

1. Do I build peace and stillness into my life? How?

2. When was the last time I set my mind free … free to be curious, to be amazed, to enjoy? If my mind is habitually caught up in self-absorption, stress, or responsibility, I need to take an oxygen mask moment.

3. Do I give myself permission to rest and to accomplish nothing? What would happen internally if I scheduled a "Do Nothing Day"? Does that thought lead me to a panic attack?

4. Do I take time to pray and meditate? Does this help to build serenity

Heart**2**Heart

1. Which of these suggestions might work for you?

2. Can you think of things that might work better for you?

3. Take out your calendar and schedule whatever needs to be scheduled.

in my life? Explain. "One of those days, Jesus went out to a mountain-side to pray, and spent the night praying to God. When morning came, he called his disciples to him and chose twelve of them, whom he also designated apostles"(Luke 6:12–13).

5. Do I ever allow myself a pamper break? Do I ever get a facial, a massage, see a movie I've been dying to see, take a long bath by candlelight, take a nap, go for coffee with a friend, get my hair done, get a manicure or a pedicure, relax with a good book, visit a park and drink in the beauty, rent two of my favorite movies and watch them both, write poetry, go to a bookstore, make love?

6. Keep a gratitude journal. Every night before you go to bed, record the blessings of the day. Joy and contentment must be welcomed and received into our life.

7. Humans were created to thrive on meaning. Get up one half-hour earlier than usual. Set the stage for the rest of your day. Thank God for a new day. Focus on the Lord. Recommit yourself to your marriage. "Today I choose to be married." Review your mission statement. Focus on three crucial questions:

   "What will my attitude be today?"

   "What will I choose to do today?"

   "How can I live out of my value system today?"

8. If I took a mental health day, what would I do?

9. What relationships do I have that sustain me? Nobody makes it alone. Treasure the friends who make your life rich and full. We all get through our tough times because someone stands in the gap with us. Who were the people who stood in the gap for you at significant times? Phone them or write them a note.

10. Renew old passions. Children take the time to try many different activities and hobbies. Adults have to make the time. Pick up on one particular passion from your childhood. Take piano lessons, try pottery, do a crossword puzzle, learn to fly a kite. Dream a little.

How did your parents relax (if they did), or how did they spend their free time (if they had any)? What messages did you receive as a kid when they found you daydreaming or goofing off? Are these voices still pushing you today?

Rate yourself on the following scale in reference to your level of spiritual connection. Where do you see yourself on this continuum? Share with your LifeMate.

Red Zone	Yellow Zone	Green Zone
Upside down.	Right side up, but feeling shaky!	Right side up and feet solidly on the ground.

How Balanced Is Our Intimate Relationship?

This chapter has focused on balance in your lifestyle. Sexual relationships also benefit tremendously from balance. Last month, as a couple, you worked together on your intimate relationship. Since we believe that this area can bring incredible joy or incredible pain to a couple, we are giving you yet another opportunity to face the sexual area together. This time each of you will be personally evaluating yourself and then discussing your findings with each other. Please do not get discouraged. The purpose of this questionnaire is to raise your awareness of the breadth of choices that influence your intimate relationship.

Assess yourself as a lover: Ask, "What do I contribute to our marriage?"

Answer the following questionnaire. Rate yourself from 1-5 on the following questions.

1	2	3	4	5
Never	Seldom	Sometimes	Frequently	Always

A. I Nurture Anticipation

Him Her

____ ____ 1. I make sexual contact a part of our daily interaction in small, playful ways.

____ ____ 2. I think of my LifeMate fondly at least once a day.

____ ____ 3. I think of emotional and sexual intimacy with my LifeMate at least once a day.

____ ____ 4. I let our sexual experiences linger in my memory.

____ ____ 5. I actively plan intentional sexual dates.

____ ____ TOTAL

B. I Am Passionately Aware

____ ____ 1. I am aware of and encourage my feelings of being sexually aroused.

____ ____ 2. When my LifeMate hugs me or kisses me, I intentionally stop my activity and respond to the affectionate advances.

____ ____ 3. I tell my LifeMate how much I look forward to shared times of intimacy.

____ ____ 4. I am aware of the atmosphere I need to maximize our love making times, and I communicate it to my LifeMate.

____ ____ 5. I am aware of what my LifeMate needs in order to enjoy our time together.

____ ____ TOTAL

C. I Enjoy My Own Body

____ ____ 1. I can forget about my "defects" and get into a state of mind where I can relax and enjoy the feel of my body.

____ ____ 2. I am at ease being nude in front of my LifeMate.

____ ____ 3. I exercise my body regularly.

____ ____ 4. I make my appearance a priority.

____ ____ 5. I am a student of my own body. I know how I need to be touched in order to be sexually aroused and I communicate that to my LifeMate.

____ ____ TOTAL

D. I Am an Intentional Romantic

____ ____ 1. I guard our bedroom. I make certain that there is a working lock on our door. I teach our children to honor a closed door. I do not argue in the bedroom. I keep the bedroom attractive.

____ ____ 2. I touch my LifeMate affectionately on a daily basis in a way that he or she enjoys and for no other purpose than being affectionate.

____ ____ 3. I am an intentional planner of date nights and weekends away.

____ ____ 4. I surprise my LifeMate occasionally by planning activities he or she would enjoy that are not necessarily my first priority.

____ ____ 5. I give cards, write letters, or choose gifts that demonstrate to my LifeMate that I am an interested student of my LifeMate.

____ ____ TOTAL

> We run faster when we have lost our way.

E. I Risk Emotional Intimacy

____ ____ 1. I let my LifeMate know what is happening in my world on a daily basis.

____ ____ 2. I demonstrate an eagerness to understand my LifeMate's world.

____ ____ 3. I admit my feelings and fear to my LifeMate.

____ ____ 4. I tell my LifeMate my needs, desires, and hopes.

____ ____ 5. I let my LifeMate know the impact his or her choices have on me.

____ ____ TOTAL

F. I Value Change

____ ____ 1. Once in a while, I surprise my LifeMate by wearing something new that he or she would find attractive.

____ ____ 2. I introduce new activities and interests to our planned date night.

____ ____ 3. I plan a weekend away without any children, family members, or friends once in a while.

____ ____ 4. I introduce new ideas, techniques, fantasies, positions or play to our intimate time together once in a while.

____ ____ 5. I suggest changes of setting and different times for our lovemaking periodically.

____ ____ TOTAL

G. I Am a Skilled Lover

____ ____ 1. I tell my LifeMate what I need and like sexually.

____ ____ 2. I make an intentional effort to learn about significant changes in my LifeMate's sexual needs and desires. I accept my LifeMate's limits.

____ ____ 3. I talk tenderly to my LifeMate while we are making love.

____ ____ 4. I follow my LifeMate's requests willingly and without taking offense.

____ ____ 5. I make love with my eyes open over 50 percent of the time that we are being sexually intimate.

H. I Talk about Our Sexual Relationship

____ ____ 1. I talk openly with my LifeMate about my sexual needs and preferences.

____ ____ 2. I make it extremely clear to my LifeMate that I enjoy specific actions and touch in our lovemaking.

____ ____ 3. I talk with my LifeMate about things I would like to change or introduce into our lovemaking.

____ ____ 4. If I turn my LifeMate down for a sexual encounter I make an alternative time for another sexual encounter that would work better for me, and I keep it.

____ ____ 5. When I am anticipating a time of lovemaking and my LifeMate isn't, I can express disappointment without pouting, withdrawing, or threatening him or her.

____ ____ TOTAL

I. I Am an Active Participant

____ ____ 1. I set aside regular time to make lovemaking a priority in our marriage.

____ ____ 2. I am able to block out mental distractions once we begin to make love.

____ ____ 3. I caress and massage my LifeMate's body.

____ ____ 4. I take pleasure in using all my senses in our lovemaking.

____ ____ 5. I initiate a time of prayer after we have made love while we are still holding each other.

____ ____ TOTAL

J. I Am a Responsible Contributing LifeMate

____ ____ 1. I confess my faults and mistakes to my LifeMate.

____ ____ 2. I take responsibility for doing specific tasks and chores willingly and regularly.

_____ _____ 3. Once in a while I surprise my LifeMate with an act of service that he or she has not asked me to perform.

_____ _____ 4. If my LifeMate needs separate time during the week to be with friends or to pursue hobbies or ministry, I facilitate that.

_____ _____ 5. I express gratitude for and to my LifeMate in front of our family and friends.

_____ _____ TOTAL

INSTRUCTIONS:

Add up the numbers in each section and record them in the blank labeled TOTAL. Then plot the separate totals on the appropriate lines on the following graph. Draw a line connecting your results. Use two different ink colors.

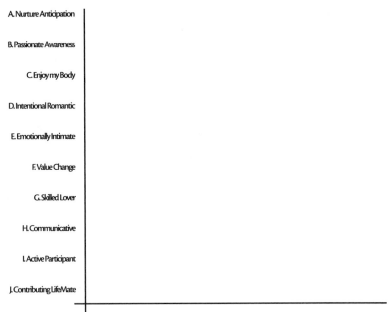

A. Nurture Anticipation

B. Passionate Awareness

C. Enjoy my Body

D. Intentional Romantic

E. Emotionally Intimate

F. Value Change

G. Skilled Lover

H. Communicative

I. Active Participant

J. Contributing LifeMate

1 2 3 4 5 6 7 8 9 10 11 12 13 14 15 16 17 18 19 20 21 22 23 24 25

Week 1: Pillow Talk

What used to be your top five favorite things to do ten years ago? Mark these with a check (√). What are your top ten favorite things now? Mark these with an "X." Each of you put your initials in the spaces that apply to you.

_____ Spending time alone

_____ Spending time with my LifeMate

_____ Spending time with friends

_____ Spending time with family

_____ Talking on the telephone

_____ Listening to music

_____ Playing music or singing

_____ Surfing the Internet

_____ Writing and reading e-mails

_____ Watching sports

_____ Watching television

_____ Going to movies

_____ Hiking

_____ Golfing

_____ Dancing

_____ Biking

_____ Making crafts

_____ Working out

_____ Playing a team sport

_____ Playing video games

_____ Shopping

_____ Traveling

_____ Playing games

_____ Reading

_____ Tinkering

_____ Eating

Heart2Heart

1. When you looked at your graph, were there any surprises? Share them with your LifeMate.

2. Discuss one of the areas in which you scored high. Take turns focusing on one of your stronger areas and talking about it. Affirm each other.

3. Now pick an area in which you scored lower than you like and begin to brainstorm what you personally and together could do to improve.

4. What three specific actions will make it obvious to your LifeMate that you are exerting intentional efforts to improve in this area?

5. Ask God to help you move closer to each other in those specific ways. Thank God for your intimate relationship.

_____ Entertaining

_____ Attending a party

_____ Going to the beach, mountains, city

_____ Extending hospitality

_____ Attending a concert

_____ Working on a hobby

_____ Going to a church event

_____ Playing with my pet

_____ Reminiscing

_____ Making love

_____ Planning a vacation or adventure

_____ Other!

Week 2: Pillow Talk

Take turns answering this question: Is our life one that we want, one that we are actively choosing, or is it just a life that pleases a lot of other people?

Week 3: Date Night

Spend an evening with a couple whom you both respect and admire. It would be great if they were ahead of you in the journey of life. Let them know ahead of time that you want to pick their brains. You might want to give them these questions before you meet. Then enjoy learning from their life journey.

1. How do you sort out the best from the good in your life personally and in your marriage?

2. How do you decide what your daily priorities are?

3. How do you make each other a priority?

4. How do you renew yourself? How do you cultivate pleasure?

5. Do you have times when you evaluate your relationship? If so, how often do you do it? Where do you do it? What meaning does it have to you both?

Week 4: Dates for Mates

Create an intimate evening together without kids. Spend an extended period of time talking to, touching, and loving each other! Every marriage needs more of this kind of balance.

FROM PREVIOUS MONTH:

I COMMIT TO MAKING OUR SEXUAL
RELATIONSHIP SATISFYING, SENSUAL,
AND SPIRITUAL.

IN MY DESIRE TO LIVE ONE GOOD YEAR OF MARRIAGE WITH MY LIFEMATE,

I COMMIT TO ESTABLISHING BALANCE IN OUR MARRIAGE.

MONTH

TWELVE

"Legacy: Leaving Behind Passivity"

> *"Remember, life is not what happens to you,*
> *but what you make of what happens to you.*
> *Everyone dies, but not everyone fully lives.*
> *Too many people are having 'near-life experiences!'"*
>
> **Anonymous**

WHEN YOU EMBRACE THE DREAM GOD has planted inside of you, when you discover your destiny, and when you watch God release his intentions through your life and in your marriage, you will feel incredibly alive! A man who resigned from his job to follow his purpose had this to say: "Soon after I resigned, I began to feel happier and more satisfied. I learned that measuring my success in terms of numbers was toxic. I also learned that true success cannot be measured through someone else's eyes. It had to evolve from my own spirit."

When we live with a daily awareness of the influence we are exerting and the legacy we are leaving, our every action and word takes on new meaning. God uses us to carry on his creative work in the lives of the people we touch. We make a difference!

A Tribute to a Man of Legacy (by Phil Callaway)

"The world slows down remarkably when a friend dies. Things you once thought important don't mean a thing. Things you worried about yesterday, vanish today. Money won't buy what you want, and sometimes you find yourself wishing for five more minutes to say what you didn't say when you knew you should have.

"Cordell Darling didn't leave things unsaid. He met you in the church foyer with welcome written on his face and encouragement all over his lips. Some people have been bitten in church parking lots. Never by Cordell. Some consider it their spiritual gift to complain about the music or the hairdos or the sermon. Cordell told you how wonderful things were. Some delight in pointing fingers at the world. Cordell told you what God was doing there. 'Awesome' was one of his favorite words. 'Fabulous' was another.

"A few days after his death, I found myself stopping to talk to children, adopting Cordell's vocabulary, encouraging people I should have encouraged long ago. I pray I will never stop. Sometimes you can measure a man's influence by the volume of cigarette butts in the church parking lot at his funeral. There were plenty at this one. Fifteen hundred people don't show up too much in a small town, but they gathered to say goodbye today. Many were 'pre-Christians,' as Cordell liked to call them. One was a Buddhist. Dozens considered Cordell their best friend. Teenagers in our town called him their mentor. He was my Prairie High School hockey coach, my cheerleader, and one of my biggest fans.

"When my wife and I were first married, Cordell took us out for lunch, hoping to sell us life insurance. And he told us that no matter what our decision, the very best life insurance policy wasn't for sale. The assurance that we can live forever with Jesus by simple faith in God is the best present we'll ever receive and free for the asking. That message has forever changed our lives.

"I wish for every church a Cordell. For every community. Every school. Every home. If something blessed him, he said so. He was human like the rest of us, but he kept pointing us higher. Cordell's golf swing needed some work, and he could barely change a light bulb, but he could light up your face with a compliment. He never met anyone who was just plain ordinary. They were always fantastic, unbelievable, or incredible. He looked past my faults and embellished my attributes. I picture him walking around heaven now, patting angels between the wings, saying, 'Wow! Good job! You're amazing! You've been doing this how many years?'

"A few months ago Cordell sat in my office, struggling to balance a busy schedule with God's will. He was worn out, and he chuckled when I told him about the book I was writing: *Who Put the World on Fast Forward?*

"'We've confused successfulness with fruitfulness,' said Cordell, staring out my third-story window. 'Success brings some rewards and maybe even fame. But real joy comes from being fruitful.'

"I'm still thinking about that."

Heart2Heart

1. What aspects of Cordell's legacy make you want to know him?

2. How do you want to be remembered?

3. How would you like your life to be different in five years?

From Dave's Journal:

Cordell was also my hockey coach. He was one of the two men who stand out in my life as the greatest influencers of who I am today. He taught me the importance of every person, the contagiousness of enthusiasm, the powerfulness of affirmation, and lived his Christian life with zest. What a legacy!

His wife, Joanne, was a gem. I remember returning from their home one evening when my parents said to me, "We hope you find someone to marry as nice as Joanne." My reply to them was, "I have."

I began to tell them about Janet Shantz, and the rest is history. Her name became Janet Congo.

From Jan's Journal:

Twenty-four years ago we had the privilege of being discipled by Ray and Anne Ortlund. The first group we were in with them was a couple's group. After that, we each individually joined women's and men's small groups with them. What a rich experience these groups were! We were loved and affirmed, pointed to Jesus, held accountable to be who we believed God wanted us to be, and given opportunities to minister. Life rubbing against life.

Ray and Anne made themselves vulnerable to us and no topic was off-limits. They used to tell us that the greatest way to stay young was to invest one's life in younger people. They believed that their influence for eternity would be extended as they invested in people who wanted to invest in others. Just being with them made us want to be more.

When our daughter, Amy, was born at four o'clock in the afternoon of May 21, 1980, they and our small group were the first people who prayed over her two and a half hours later. They modeled team teaching for us and we learned. They took us along on ministry opportunities. We watched and we learned. They loved each other enthusiastically and openly. We learned. They wrote books that we devoured. Over the years there have been the shared dinners full of love and laughter. They always wanted to know how we were doing with Jesus and each other. Yes, they were interested in what we were doing, but that always seemed secondary, and we learned. Life rubbing against life. As a result we learned.

Don't be afraid to go out on a limb.
That's where the fruit is!

H. Jackson Brown
(Klein, Winning Words,
Portland House, p. 96)

Under What Influence?

A priest was confronted by a soldier while he was walking down a road in pre-revolutionary Russia. The soldier, aiming his rifle at the priest, commanded, "Who are You? … Where are you going? … Why are you going there?"

Unfazed, the priest calmly replied, "How much do they pay you?"

Somewhat surprised the soldier responded, "Twenty-five kopecks a month."

The priest paused and in a deeply thoughtful manner said, "I have a proposal for you. I'll pay you fifty kopecks each month if you stop me here every day and challenge me to respond to those same three questions."[1]

If we seek to influence others, we must be willing to be influenced. We must move beyond transparency to vulnerability. Transparency is under our control. We decide what to share, when, and how to share it. Vulnerability is out of our control. We submit ourselves to someone, someone who has access to all of us, our strengths, and our weaknesses. When we give access to our life we allow this somebody to know us and to influence us.

> Submission is a love word, not a control word to be
> slapped on others like a choke collar. Submission means
> letting someone love us, teach us, or influence us. In
> fact, the degree to which we submit to others is the
> degree to which we experience their love, regardless of
> how much they love us.[2]

Jesus was a follower first and a leader second. He followed God the Father with all his heart, soul, and mind. Jesus sought out God's will. He withdrew from the crowds to hear it. He submitted to it. As a result, when Christ led, he led with integrity.

What about you? Do you have someone in your life who will tell you the truth, who will keep you grounded, and who helps keep things in perspective? Do you have someone who will receive your truth without jeopardizing your friendship? To whom are you accountable? Does anyone really know you?

Community is the context for character development. Problems in life are a direct result of sowing one thing and expecting to reap something entirely different. We must commit time and effort to develop truth in our innermost being. Uncompromising character development produces profound influence. It's so easy to be surrounded by people and yet not be personally known by anyone in particular. It's too easy to live a lie.

Nathaniel Branden, author of *Six Pillars of Self-Esteem*, wrote in the March 1997 issue of *Personal Excellence* magazine:

> We live a lie when we misrepresent the reality of our experience or the truth of our being. I am living a lie when I pretend a love I do not feel; when I pretend an indifference I do not feel; when I present myself as more than I am; when I say I am angry, and the truth is I am afraid; when I pretend to be helpless, and the truth is I am manipulative; when I deny and conceal my excitement about life; when I affect a blindness that denies my awareness; when I affect a knowledge I do not possess; when I laugh when I need to cry; when I spend unnecessary time with people I dislike; when I present myself as the embodiment of values I do not feel or hold; when I am kind to everyone except those I profess to love; when I fake beliefs to win acceptance; when I fake modesty; when I fake arrogance; when I allow my silence to imply agreement with convictions I do not share."

Other people often know when we are faking it. At times another's insights may be more than we wish to assimilate. Since we don't just want to talk the walk, we want to walk the walk, we need a collaborative push toward growth. This takes a consistent, long-term willingness to submit ourselves to the feedback and influence of others.

Periodically we need to question ourselves: Is the influence I am exerting arising from my character, from the essence of who I am, and from what I believe? Or is it coming from an external image I have designed to protect me from my fears, limitations, and inadequacies? Am

I more invested in looking good or in being authentic? People often ask, "What are you going to be when you grow up?" A more appropriate question would be, "Who are you going to be when you grow up?"

Instructed by Life's Ups and Downs

Each of us must be willing to get rid of the life we expected so as to experience the life that is waiting for us. Whether we like our life as it is, or wish for change, nothing stays the same. Each of us must get to the point where we let go of what we once knew. We must release what used to be for what can be. Sometimes the strengths that have been tremendously useful up to this point in time may get in the way as life changes.

Karl Wallenda's final high-wire performance was an attempt to cross the space between two tall buildings. As he inched his way across using his famous balancing pole, an intense wind came up. He was in immediate danger. As the wind blew him off the wire, he clutched onto his balancing pole. He needed to let go of the pole and grab the wire. He didn't. He clutched the pole that had saved his balance so many times before. He held onto the familiar when it no longer served him and ended up plunging to his death.

The fact that we must walk into the unknown requires us to release the familiar while facing possible difficulties and failures. A paradox of life is that success only happens after we have risked failure. Frankly, if we only experience success, very few will seek our influence.

Michael Caine, the actor, was asked if he had any fatherly advice for his two daughters. His reply was profound:

Heart2Heart

1. When in your life have you welcomed honest appraisals and feedback?

2. How do you demonstrate your willingness to learn from others and to submit to others?

3. Who have been the major influencers in your life? This list can include people, living or dead, people who you knew intimately or just through books or movies. These people create a patchwork quilt of influence in your life.

There's a motto I got from a producer in repertory the-
atre. I was in rehearsals, waiting behind a door to come
out while a couple onstage were having a row. They
started throwing furniture, and a chair lodged in front
of the door. My cue came and I could only get halfway
in. I stopped and said, "I can't get in. The chair's in the
way." And the producer said, "Use the difficulty." I said,
"What do you mean? And he said, "Well, if it's a drama,
pick it up and smash it. If it's a comedy, fall over it." This
idea stuck in my mind, and I taught it to my children—
that in any situation in life that seems negative, there is
something positive you can do with it. "Use the difficulty." It's a motto in our family.[3]

Notice life's ups and downs. Enjoy the successes and learn from the
failures. Don't identify with either. They are both temporary. When we
identify with life's ups and downs, we either become
proud or we become a victim. Neither stance serves us
well. In order to leave a profound legacy we need to be
a continual learner.

A life without purpose is an early death.

Goethe
(Cashman, Levin, Leadership
From the Inside Out,
Executive Excellence
Publishing, Provo, Utah.
1999, p.67)

"Praise be to the God and Father of our Lord
Jesus Christ, the Father of compassion and the
God of all comfort, who comforts us in all our
troubles, so that we can comfort those in any
trouble with the comfort we ourselves have
received from God." (2 Cor. 1:3–4)

Ignited by Purpose

"It is a dangerous business to arrive in eternity with possibilities which one himself has prevented from
becoming actualities. Possibility is a hint from God. A

person must follow it ... if God does not want it, then let Him hinder it; the person must not hinder it himself."
Soren Kierkegaard[4]

Are you living your life as if you are on a treadmill going nowhere? Are you content just watching others live? God wants you to believe that you matter to him. He has a plan for your life. He has a plan for your marriage.

Many of us desire to lead a life of meaning and contribution, yet we don't know where to begin. We often feel as if we are playing the concerto of life with one finger.

In their brilliant book, *First Things First,* Stephen Covey and Roger and Rebecca Merrill make a distinction between two powerful tools in our lives, the clock and the compass.[5] The clock represents our schedules, goals, and activities. The compass represents our vision, values, principles, and purpose. Problems arise when we sense a gap between the clock and the compass—when our actions and activities don't contribute to our purpose.

Heart2Heart

1. When you were in your early twenties, what did you think you'd be doing at this stage of life? How is your life different?

2. How have you personally grown through failures, losses, and disappointments? Give examples.

3. Has there been a time in your life when a loss actually opened you up to a new opportunity? Be specific. Has failure ever turned out to be the beginning of a new story and not the end? Explain.

We are most lost as human beings when we lose connection to our principles, beliefs, and values. On the journey to discovering our purpose, we need to ask ourselves, "What do I really enjoy doing? What energizes and excites me? What gives my life meaning?"

Purpose always serves. It always makes a difference. It adds value to others. It happens in the context of relationship. The Dead Sea is dead only because it takes in water and doesn't give any out. It is constipated. A person or a marriage without purpose is like the Dead Sea. We all have been blessed in order to be a blessing.

Our purpose helps us to integrate our hearts with our hands, our daily lives with our dreams, and our capabilities with our character. Our purpose is constant. The manifestation of it is not. Our purpose helps us align our life to our value system on a daily basis.

Live on Purpose

In order to live on purpose, we don't have to be independently wealthy, we don't have to quit our day jobs, and we don't have to give away all our material possessions, unless God asks that of us. What we must do is focus our energy and efforts in the direction of our purpose, whether on or off the job.

One of our partners in LifeMates is Mike Keyes. Over the years he has kept a journal of quotes, clever ideas, and messages that grabbed his heart and mind. He is now putting them on the computer under specific themes. Why? So that he can present it as a gift to his daughters when they become adults.

Grandparents whose children and grandchildren moved to the opposite coast of the United States racked their brains for how to best maintain a long-term relationship. Their solution was brilliant. Once a month they visited a bookstore and bought four children's books in duplicate. They carefully wrapped a set of each of the books and then sent them off in a package. Every Wednesday at 7:30 p.m. they would phone their grandchildren, who were in their pajamas, sitting on Mom and Dad's bed waiting for a call from Grandma and Grandpa. The grandparents would talk to the little ones and then at some point the grandchildren would open one package. Grandma and Grandpa would then read them the new story. As the years passed the tables turned and the grandchildren started to read the new book to their grandparents.

Empower yourself. Take a Red Cross class in anything from the Heimlich maneuver to CPR to lifeguarding. Visit redcross.org. One of our friends gives one week a year to lifeguard at a camp for at-risk children run by ex-convicts. He tells us it's one of the most meaningful things he does all year.

Friends of Dave's family, Jack and Belle Tattersoll, are both ninety-one years of age. Jack is a talented carpenter. He makes wooden toys for children. His wife helps paint them. They sell these toys. They take the money and support forty orphans in Guatemala. What are you going to do when you grow up?

Friends of ours, Dr. Paul and Lois Ferris, a brilliant couple who minister out of Bethel Seminary, got their extended family together for two weeks in July 2002. They outfitted their backyard with an inflated swimming pool, a Slip-n-Slide®, swings, and "grandstand seats" for a very special project. Paul had promised the grandkids that they could help him build a playhouse. Paul designed it. Starting the project was part of that summer's vacation adventure. It's named "Londonderry Cottage" after Londonderry, Ireland where Mom Ferris's parents were born. It is a thatched-roof cottage. The grandkids, all preschoolers, helped put up the walls and hammered. They plan to decorate this next summer.

Find a fulfilling way to volunteer. Take one lunch hour a week to teach an adult or a child how to read. Volunteer at a hospital, a senior center, through Big Brothers/Big Sisters or Special Olympics. Become a mentor or coach. Teach a class or lead a support group. Go on a missions trip. Help at a soup kitchen. Build a home through Habitat for Humanity (800-422-4828). Donate time to a favorite charity. Volunteer at a museum, art gallery, library, hospital, or theater. The American Hiking Society needs people to fix deteriorating trails at national parks (americanhiking.org). Volunteer to help at your church. Get to know your neighbors. Invite them over for a barbecue. Donate your used books to a preschool, library, or book pool.

Friends of our decided that when their grandchildren turned thirteen, they could, with a friend of their choosing, take a trip with their grandparents anywhere they would like to go in the world. (Our parameters would not be quite so broad.) The entire trip was planned around the grandchild's interests. The grandparents told us that it was an invaluable way of getting to know each grandchild. The grandchildren were one step ahead of the grandparents, though. Since they could bring one friend, they chose to bring a cousin, so that each of them would end up with two fabulous trips with Grandpa and Grandma.

Take thirty seconds to make a difference. Every time you click on hungersite.com, sponsors will donate food to the hungry; for every click on the breastcancersite.com, a woman in need will get a free mammogram.

Do an unexpected act of kindness. Let someone else have your parking spot. Put a quarter in someone's parking meter that is about to expire. Write a former teacher of yours or of your children's to say thanks. If a waiter or waitress does a great job, tip them and tell their boss. Give a salesperson your full attention. If you have a friend going through a difficult time, do a practical act of kindness. Cut grass, shovel snow, clean house, go shopping, or take over a meal.

During our last year of graduate school, we didn't have two nickels to rub together. Once a month an envelope with a Bible verse and a crisp $100 bill would appear. To this day we have no idea who gave us that much-needed money.

Heart2Heart

1. Which of these suggestions appeal to you?

2. Can you think of others who have influenced you through their example?

3. Can you think of any other ways you would like to contribute to planet earth?

Inspiring One Another's Purpose

Distanced couples look in opposite directions. Enmeshed couples lose themselves in each other's eyes. Purposeful couples look outward in the same direction. That doesn't mean they are necessarily doing the same thing. What it does mean, is that they are both committed to encouraging and facilitating each other to be all that they can be. Just like Michelangelo, love sees in our LifeMate the angel yet to be carved from the stone.

Carl Jung once said that the second half of life is meant to explore the things that we missed in the first. It seems that at one point in our life we rushed out to change the world, but often and unfortunately, the world changed us. We gave up our dream. We forgot our purpose.

No one can neglect his or her purpose without detrimental consequences.

It is not true there can only be one purpose in a marriage. Marriage is not enough for personal fulfillment. Money, status, and power do not give meaning to life. The huge question facing each couple is how can we make two dreams come true without sacrificing our relationship, our family, or our sanity? Each couple has two sets of talents that need to be exercised for the good of others.

The earlier in a marriage that we make two purposes a top priority, the better. If you don't have children, it's easier. Yet, when they are in the picture, children benefit from quality time with two parents who are fulfilled as a result of being true to their purpose.

The process of embracing two dreams may take a three-, five-, or even a ten-year plan. It takes commitment, coordination, and an investment of time and resources. It may require setting aside something that would be more fun to do. It requires that we face our fears. It always requires letting go of what "should be" and serving the other.

"For we are God's workmanship, created in Christ Jesus to do good works, which God prepared in advance for us to do."

Ephesians 2:10

David thought he was marrying a kindergarten teacher who would support his seminary education. Jan thought she was marrying a minister. Life's divinely ordained curve balls and our divinely inspired dreams changed that. We've learned in more than thirty years of marriage that when there are two wills, two loving hearts, and a support system, there always is a way. We must be partners in creativity or we risk depression that comes with the death of one of our dreams. In order to be true to ourselves, what we believe our purpose is and what we do must be in harmony.

Eugene Peterson writes in *Run with the Horses* about a family of swallows learning to fly. As they perched on a dead limb stretching over a lake, the parent began nudging them toward the end of the branch. One by one they were pushed off and thus the chicks learned how to fly! The last little swallow was not about to be bullied, and he grasped the branch, but loose enough so he swung around, obstinately landing upside down! The unperturbed adult pecked at the young bird's clinging talons until it became so uncomfortable the swallow released his grip and those wings began to pump. Now the whole family was able to do what God had designed them to do best ... fly!

While birds have feet and can walk, they are best at flying! Not until they learn to fly do they live as God intended them to live! Has your marriage partnership helped you soar? Has marriage meant that you had to abandon a dream, or has it helped you embrace your dream? The dual-purpose marriage affirms that it is in the spending of oneself that one becomes rich.

Ponder these questions personally and with your support people:

1. What do you want to accomplish in the next ten years?

2. What do you most want to learn? Make a list.

3. What skills do you want to develop? Make a list.

4. Who would you most like to meet? Where would you most like to go? Make a list.

5. Complete this sentence: I feel most energetic and alive when I ...

6. What have you always wanted to do but never allowed yourself to do because it was too expensive, too reckless, or would be too complicated?

Heart2Heart

1. Is there something special that you're meant to contribute to the world? How does your LifeMate support your quest for purpose? What does this mean to you personally? What does it mean to your relationship?

2. How do you support your LifeMate's quest for purpose? How does this affect your intimacy?

3. How could you make it possible for each other to pursue purpose in life based on what brings you the most joy? How could you then use it to serve others?

We create a legacy one day at a time, one moment at a time. We need to ask ourselves, "How do I show up for life? What is it like to be married to me? What is it like to be my child? What is it like to be my friend?"

If, as a result of being in relationship with me, people are afraid, angry, stressed, hurt, or frustrated, I need to look into the mirror! On a weekly basis we need to take a "Search Me, O God" personal evaluation. Do this as a gift to those you love.

"Search Me, O God" Personal Evaluation

A. During the past week, to what degree (1 being low and 10 being high) have I operated out of my God-given value system? If you are incredibly courageous, you can ask your LifeMate to rate you after you have rated yourself. Compare ratings.

_____ 1. Have I honored my commitments?

_____ 2. Have I expressed words of affirmation?

_____ 3. Have I demonstrated kindness through my actions and in my attitudes?

_____ 4. Have I expressed gratitude through word or deed?

_____ 5. Have I talked to and about others respectfully and politely?

_____ 6. Have I been generous in my spirit and in my actions?

_____ 7. Have I rejoiced with those who rejoice?

_____ 8. Have I wept with those who weep? Have I demonstrated empathy and compassion?

_____ 9. Have I done a quiet act of service for someone that wasn't required of me?

_____ 10. Have I listened to understand in a conflictive situation?

_____ 11. Have I asked someone to forgive me if needed?

_____ 12. Have I offered forgiveness to someone?

_____ 13. Have I spoken my truth in love?

_____ 14. Have I trusted someone else?

_____ 15. Have I been a person of my word?

_____ 16. Have I brought joy to those in my sphere of influence?

_____ 17. Have I worshiped and fellowshipped with the God of the universe?

_____ 18. Have I submitted to sound counsel?

_____ 19. Have I made someone laugh?

_____ 20. Have I left my world a little better than I found it?

_____ 21. Have I demonstrated courage by sticking with my convictions?

_____ 22. Have I exercised self-discipline in my words and actions?

_____ 23. Have I taken initiative and been proactive?

_____ 24. Have I demonstrated loyalty?

_____ 25. Have I kept eternity forefront in my mind?

B. Do I need to go to my LifeMate and my children to apologize for anything? Do I need to go to God? Do I need to talk to my support person?

C. What area do I need to work on this next week? How might I be intentional about that?

Jim Collins, in his business book *Good to Great*,[6] looks at the leadership style that makes organizations thrive. One of the characteristics of top level leaders is that in times of crisis, they look in the mirror and take responsibility for poor results. They don't blame other people, external factors, or bad luck. In successful times this same leader looks out the window to other people, to external factors, and to good luck as causes of the company's success. We think this mirror and window principle would work well in marriages, too.

The values that we live by create the world we live in. Each of us becomes what we choose to be moment by moment. We must judge our success, not by what we have acquired, but by who we have become. Search me, O God!

Expand your influence by:

- Mending a quarrel
- Seeking out a forgotten friend
- Writing a long overdue love note
- Hugging someone tightly and whispering, "I love you"
- Forgiving an enemy
- Being gentle and patient with an angry person
- Expressing appreciation
- Gladdening the heart of a child
- Finding the time to keep a promise
- Releasing a grudge
- Listening
- Speaking kindly to a stranger
- Entering into another's sorrow
- Smiling, laughing a little
- Taking a walk with a friend
- Lessening your demands on others
- Apologizing if you were wrong
- Turning off the television and talking
- Praying for someone who helped you when you hurt
- Encouraging someone

Rate yourself on how intentional you are about the legacy you're leaving.

Red Zone	Yellow Zone	Green Zone
I'm unaware of my influence. I am not concerned about my legacy.	I'm becoming aware of my influence. I'm beginning to think about my legacy.	I am aware of my influence. I am intentional about my legacy.

Quality couples long to be in relationship with a LifeMate whose vision is higher that their next paycheck. All thriving couples have a dream higher than the attainment of the American Dream.

Your marriage has the power to change your world and the world at large. We believe that God created marriage as a base for ministering to others and to point others to God. Whenever together you transcend the boundaries of your own marriage to minister to someone else, it cultivates the sense of being LifeMates as little else does.

By spending a year of your life working together through this book, you have together created an intentional marriage. You have divorced the way you used to do marriage. You have left old unproductive patterns behind, started over, and created One Good Year with your LifeMate. In the process you have impacted those in your circle of influence. You have left a most unusual legacy in a world of throw-away marriages.

We commend you! We congratulate you! We pray for you! Now that you have lived out One Good Year, repeat it next year and every year that follows. May if be said of you that you didn't get married for "better or worse," you got married for "better and better."

Become a LifeMate one day at a time, one choice at a time. Keep growing! Keep moving toward love! Make your marriage a work of art—a work in progress. Never lose sight of the fact that you are leaving a legacy!

Week 1: Pillow Talk

When John Goddard was 15 years of age, he wrote a life list of 127 goals. He wanted to explore the Nile, Amazon, and Congo rivers; climb Mount Everest and Mount Kilimanjaro; ride an elephant, ostrich, and bronco; retrace Marco Polo's travels. He wanted to read the Bible, all of Shakespeare, Plato, Aristotle, and an entire encyclopedia. He wanted to visit every country in the world and he wanted to write a book. At the age of 68, he had achieved 114 of his goals.

Together, create a list of things you would like to do and places you would like to visit before you die. Make a long list. Dream a little together.

Week 2: Pillow talk

If we were to write a letter to our children or to a valued child on what is most important in life, what would we tell them? Create such a letter to give to that person when they turn eighteen.

Week 3: Pillow Talk

Complete these thoughts:

One of my favorite books was …

One of my all-time favorite movies was …

One of the best trips I ever took was …

One of the most influential experiences I ever had was …

One of the people who influenced me the most was …

One of my heroes growing up was …

A defining spiritual moment in my life was …

One of the best classes I ever attended was …

One of the things I am most proud of is …

Week 4: Pillow Talk

Answer these questions:

What do I value most?

What in my life is trivial and what is essential?

What type of person do I want to be?

FROM PREVIOUS MONTH:
I COMMIT TO ESTABLISHING BALANCE IN
OUR MARRIAGE.

**IN MY DESIRE TO LIVE ONE GOOD YEAR
OF MARRIAGE WITH MY LIFEMATE,**

I COMMIT TO LEAVING A SIGNIFICANT AND
ETERNAL LEGACY!

For information about Dr. David and Janet Congo and LifeMates
ministry, speaking engagements, and resources contact:

Dr. David and Janet Congo
23441 South Pointe Drive, Suite 180
Laguna Hills, CA 92653
Phone: Lisa Keyes, LifeMates Company
949-859-5937
www.eLifeMates.com

NOTES

Month #1
1. C. S. Lewis, *The Four Loves* (New York: Harcourt Brace, 1960), 183.
2. Sam Horn, *Tongue Fu* (New York: St Martin's Press, 1996), 48.

Month #2
1. Allen Klein, *Winning Words* (New York: Portland House, 2002), 162.
2. Gregory Godek, *Love, The Course They Forgot to Teach You in School* (Naperville, Ill.: Casablanca Press, 1997), 37.
3. Ibid., 38.
4. John C. Maxwell, *The 17 Essential Qualities of a Team Player: Becoming the Kind of Player Every Team Wants* (Nashville: Thomas Nelson Publishers, 2002), 87, 88.

Month #3
1. Henry Cloud and John Townsend, *How People Grow* (Grand Rapids: Zondervan, 2001), 161.
2. Ronald Schwartz, *The 501 Best and Worst Things Ever Said About Marriage* (New York: Citadel Press, 1995), 49.

Month#4
1. David Augsburger, *Caring Enough to Forgive* (Ventura, Calif.: Regal Books,1981), 26.

Month #5
1. John C. Maxwell, *The 17 Essential Qualities of a Team Player: Becoming the Kind of Player Every Team Wants* (Nashville: Thomas Nelson Publishers, 2002), 80.

Month #6
1. Hugh and Gail Prather, *Only If We Are: Notes to Each Other* (New York: Bantam Books, 2000), 10.
2. James Dobson, *Love Must Be Tough* (Waco, Tex.: Word Publishing, 1996), 196.
3. Harriet Lerner, *The Dance of Connection* (New York: Harper Collins, 2001), 91.
4. Henry Cloud and John Townsend, *Boundaries in Marriage* (Grand Rapids: Zondervan, 1999).

Month #7
1. Joel Goodman, *Laffirmations* (Deerfield Beach, Fla.: Health Communications Inc., 1995), 198.
2. Maggie Fox, "Just Anticipating Merriment Cuts Stress" (*Orange County Register* Focus/Health, 7 November 1992), 15.
3. Comparisons were sparked by an article by Martha Beck in *O, the Oprah Magazine* (May 2002), entitled, "The Clue is in Your Funpoint", 224.
4. Gregory Godek, *Romantic Mischief* (Naperville, Ill.: Casablanca Press, 1997), 113.

Month #8

1. Sharon Boorstin, "Cooking Up A New Life", *More Magazine* (March 2003), 114.
2. John C. Maxwell, *The 17 Essential Qualities of a Team Player: Becoming the Kind of Player Every Team Wants*, (New York: Free Press, 2001).

Month #9

1. Allen Klein, ed., *Winning Words* (New York: Portland House, 2002), 406.
2. Lee and Leslie Strobel, *Surviving A Spiritual Mismatch* (Grand Rapids, Mich:, Zondervan), 62–65.
3. Charlie and Martha Shedd, *Celebration in the Bedroom* (Waco, Tex: Word, 1985), 94–98.
4. Sharon Drury, "From Tournier to T. V. Guide," *Partnership Magazine* (July/August, 1986), 42.
5. William H. Kinnaird, *Comes with the Morning* (Waco, Tex.: Word, 1979), 123.
6. Karen O'Connor, "Walking With Purpose," *Marriage Partnership* (Spring 2003).
7. Elizabeth Cody Newenhuyse, "Faith," *Marriage Partnership* (Winter, 1990), 35–37.

Month #10

1. The idea for this illustration came from: Charlotte Davis Kasl, *Women, Sex, and Addiction* (New York: Houghton Mifflin, 1989).
2. Cliff and Joyce Penner, *The Gift of Sex: A Christian Guide to Sexual Fulfillment* (Garden City: Doubleday, 1997).
3. Charlie and Martha Shedd, *Celebration in the Bedroom* (Waco, Tex.: Word, 1985), 94–98.
4. Judith Reichman, M.D., *I'm Not in the Mood: What Every Woman Should Know About Improving Her Libido* (New York: Harper, 1999). Dr. Reichman offers a concise list of the tests she recommends that assess levels of free testosterone:
>   Thyroid function (TSH, thyroid-stimulating hormone)
>   Complete blood count to rule out anemia
>   Prolactin level measurement
>   Liver function
>   Cholesterel and lipid profile
>   DHEAS (dihydroepiandrosterone) levels
>   FSH (follicle- stimulating hormone)
>   There are undesirable side effects to taking testosterone. Research them carefully and then make an educated choice.
5. Pat Love, "What is This Thing Called Love?" *Family Therapy Networker* (March/April, 1999).

Month #11

1. Herbert Benson, M.D. and William Proctor have written a thought provoking book called, *The Break Out Principle* (New York: Scribner, 2003).
2. Terry Orlick, *In Pursuit of Excellence*, Champaign, Ill.: Leisure Press, 1990), 179.

Month #12

1. Kevin Cashman, *Leadership From the Inside Out*, (Provo, Utah: Executive Excellence Publishing, 1999), 31.
2. Bill Thrall, Ken McElrath, and Bruce McNicol, *Beyond the Best* (San Francisco, Calif.: Jossey Bass, 2003), 73.
3. Lawrence Eisenberg, "Caine Scrutiny," *AARP Magazine* (May/June 2003), 53.
4. Bill Thrall, Ken McElrath, and Bruce McNicol, *Beyond the Best* (San Francisco, Calif.: Jossey Bass, 2003), 55.
5. Stephen Covey, A. Roger Merrill, and Rebecca Merrill, *First Things First* (New York, Simon & Schuster, 1996).
6. Jim Collins, *Good to Great: Why Some Companies Make the Leap and Others Don't* (New York: Harper Collins, 2001).

The Word at Work . . .

*W*hat would you do if you wanted to share God's love with children on the streets of your city? That's the dilemma David C. Cook faced in 1870s Chicago. His answer was to create literature that would capture children's hearts.

Out of those humble beginnings grew a worldwide ministry that has used literature to proclaim God's love and disciple generation after generation. Cook Communications Ministries is committed to personal discipleship—to helping people of all ages learn God's Word, embrace his salvation, walk in his ways, and minister in his name.

Opportunities—and Crisis

We live in a land of plenty—including plenty of Christian literature! But what about the rest of the world? Jesus commanded, "Go and make disciples of all nations" (Matt. 28:19) and we want to obey this commandment. But how does a publishing organization "go" into all the world?

There are five times as many Christians around the world as there are in North America. Christian workers in many of these countries have no more than a New Testament, or perhaps a single shared copy of the Bible, from which to learn and teach.

We are committed to sharing what God has given us with such Christians.

A vital part of Cook Communications Ministries is our international outreach, Cook Communications Ministries International (CCMI). Your purchase of this book, and of other books and Christian-growth products from Cook, enables CCMI to provide Bibles and Christian literature to people in more than 150 languages in 65 countries.

Cook Communications Ministries is a not-for-profit, self-supporting organization. Revenues from sales of our books, Bible curriculum, and other church and home products not only fund our U.S. ministry, but also fund our CCMI ministry around the world. One hundred percent of donations to CCMI go to our international literature programs.

... Around the World

CCMI reaches out internationally in three ways:

• Our premier International Christian Publishing Institute (ICPI) trains leaders from nationally led publishing houses around the world to develop evangelism and discipleship materials to transform lives in their countries.

• We provide literature for pastors, evangelists, and Christian workers in their national language. We provide study helps for pastors and lay leaders in many parts of the world, such as China, India, Cuba, Iran, and Vietnam.

• We reach people at risk—refugees, AIDS victims, street children, and famine victims—with God's Word. CCMI puts literature that shares the Good News into the hands of people at spiritual risk—people who might die before they hear the name of Jesus and are transformed by his love.

Word Power—God's Power

Faith Kidz, RiverOak, Honor, Life Journey, Victor, NexGen — every time you purchase a book produced by Cook Communications Ministries, you not only meet a vital personal need in your life or in the life of someone you love, but you're also a part of ministering to José in Colombia, Humberto in Chile, Gousa in India, or Lidiane in Brazil. You help make it possible for a pastor in China, a child in Peru, or a mother in West Africa to enjoy a life-changing book. And because you helped, children and adults around the world are learning God's Word and walking in his ways.

Thank you for your partnership in helping to disciple the world. May God bless you with the power of his Word in your life.

For more information about our international ministries, visit www.ccmi.org.